MW00416743

Love Your Cross

LOVE YOUR CROSS

How Suffering Becomes Sacrifice

Therese M. Williams

TAN Books
Charlotte, North Carolina

Edited by Brian Gallagher

Cover design by Caroline K. Green

Library of Congress Control Number: 2019939295

ISBN: 978-1-5051-1411-9

Published in the United States by
TAN Books
PO Box 410487
Charlotte, NC 28241
www.TANBooks.com

Printed in the United States of America

*To my mother and father, who dedicated their lives
to caring for me for forty years. Thank you for giving
me life and the gift of my Catholic Faith.*

*Also, a special thanks to Father Marian, Father Maurice, and
Father Peter for inspiring me to write this book.*

CONTENTS

FOREWORD

The Christian must always keep his eyes fixed on the Lord Jesus. Knowing that he is risen from the dead and has conquered sin and death is a tremendous encouragement to us. But keeping our eyes on the Lord in this life means that we must also be willing to suffer with him. The Lord's exhortation to "take up our cross daily and follow him" is our compass throughout our lives to make sure we are on the narrow path that leads to salvation.

Therese Williams's life has been one that is daily formed by the cross into something beautiful, and an inspiration to those who know her. I have known her my whole life. I am her brother and her godfather. Our lives have been intertwined since she came into our family in October of 1974, and she continues to influence and inspire me in my priestly vocation today.

Although I know her story, and was to some degree a part of it, I thoroughly enjoyed reading the stories of her life and seeing how she applies them in her relationship with God. The cross and suffering is something everyone knows something about. Therese helps us understand the meaning and purpose of our suffering. I also think any reader will be intrigued by the stories of Therese's life and how real joy can touch those who have been immersed in suffering.

Father Peter Williams, February 2019

LENT OF 1976

*"It's true, I suffer a great deal—but do I
suffer well? That is the question."*

—St. Thérèse of Lisieux, *Her Last Conversations*

What better sign of Christ's love is there than the cross?
Many of us go about our day surrounded by crosses.
They are nailed to the walls of our homes, suspended above
our altars, and hanging from the ends of the rosaries in our
pockets. In fact, the cross is most likely the most frequent
and common religious image we encounter each day. But
with so many crosses around us, how often do we really
contemplate the cross? How often do we stop what we are
doing, turn our eyes to it in veneration, and reflect upon its
significance?

The crosses we bear vary in size and kind because they
were uniquely made for us. We must remember that our
crosses are part of God's incredible design and he has chosen them for us from the day we were born. The question

becomes: what are we going to do with our cross? Will we lift it and walk the path of Calvary by Christ's example? Or will we allow self-pity to weigh it down until it crushes us? I contend with this very question regarding my handicap and other aspects of my life. To bear our cross is certainly a task that is easier said than done, but gazing upon Christ's cross gives us a grander perspective. That sacred artifact allows us to see the purpose of our own cross, and once we see that purpose, it becomes much easier to bear.

When I was eighteen months old, I contracted spinal meningitis. For as long as I can remember, I have been a quadriplegic in need of constant care. That's well over forty years now. I have had constant respiratory issues, severe scoliosis, and still sleep in a modern equivalent of an iron lung every night, just to be able to breathe properly. From the earliest moments of contracting my disease, God was preparing the soil of my soul for the journey ahead in living out the life of a handicapped woman.

On Thursday, March 11, 1976, my mother discovered a pox mark on my face and took me to the doctor. All signs pointed to a mild case of chickenpox. Two days later, I awoke with a dangerously high fever of 105 degrees. The doctor could detect nothing out of the ordinary and again sent me home, this time with a baby aspirin. As it was told to me, I was up and down all that night, restless, struggling with the fever. On Sunday morning, my sister, Kathy, found Mom holding me, still in her pajamas.

"Mom, are you going to church?" she asked. Instead of responding, my mom just stood there, watching my face, gazing with intent concern and worry at her struggling baby. She finally spoke. "I think we need to go back to the doctor."

Deciding to hold off until after Mass, Dad took my brothers and sisters to church while Mom stayed home with me. When Dad returned, I was in convulsions. A simple case of the chickenpox had magnified into something much greater. I was having a seizure. My mother and Kathy stood over me, frantically yelling, "Wake up, Therese! It's okay, wake up!" Terrified, my parents rushed me to the hospital.

Upon assessing me, the doctors immediately called for a spinal tap. Knowing that only Mom had the ability to calm me, they allowed her to remain in the room during the procedure. It is an extremely painful test, requiring a long needle to be inserted into the spine in order to extract fluid for lab work, so much of their success depended on Mom keeping me still. Being a scared little toddler, I made their job very difficult as I thrashed back and forth, screaming in pain.

Although spinal tap results are only available after culturing the fluid for several days, the doctors were so certain I had contracted spinal meningitis as a secondary infection to the chickenpox that antibiotic treatment began immediately. A few days later, the diagnosis was confirmed: it was bacterial meningitis.

On Sunday night, while still in the hospital, I had another seizure, stopped breathing, and went into a coma. The doctors gave me CPR, pumping air into my lungs. I was then transferred to Children's Memorial Hospital in Chicago, thirty miles away, where they had a children's respirator. It was a positive pressure respirator, which had a tube that attached to my lungs through my nose to help me breathe.

After being on this respirator for two months, the bone in my nose had eroded, making it necessary for doctors to perform a tracheotomy on me.

After the doctors had done a tracheotomy to facilitate my breathing, I began to have incidents when my pulse would slowly begin dropping and my heart rate would slow down. One day, my pulse descended relentlessly until my heart stopped altogether. Simultaneously, I stopped breathing. The intensive care nurses sounded an alarm calling for emergency aid and chased my parents out of the ICU. Doctors rushed in, attempting to get my heart started again. In the wake of heart failure is a feeling of helplessness and panic, when the loved ones present realize the fragility of life and their inability to intervene. My parents could do nothing but rely on our Lady's intercession once again. After a few anxious minutes, my heart regained its function and the crisis passed.

My parents went home from the hospital totally exhausted, physically and emotionally. No one spoke at the dinner table that night, but ate their meal quietly, listening to God in their own hearts. The weight of the emotions that hung in the room created an intensely solemn mood. Then, shattering their stupor, the telephone rang, and my brother rose to answer it. Eleven-year-old Chris then told Mom that there was a nun on the phone asking for her and saying, "Mother Teresa of Calcutta wants to speak to you."

Mom grasped the phone while Dad listened on the other line. The strong, quiet voice in the speaker was indeed the holy sister, Mother Teresa herself. She reassured Mom, "Mrs. Williams, you are not to worry; Therese is in our Blessed

Mother's hands." She told Mom that she would stop by the hospital the next morning and drop off a miraculous medal for me. My parents had not known that Mother Teresa was in Chicago, and as they had an unlisted phone number, they had no idea how Mother Teresa had obtained their number or who had asked her to call. Nevertheless, they found the medal by my bedside the following day, just as she had promised. It was as if an angel from God had phoned to reassure them that he had heard their prayers.

On April 13, 1976 during Holy Week, we were granted an Easter miracle when I took three little breaths on my own. I like to think of it as my personal expression of the Resurrection when the Holy Spirit, quite literally, breathed new life into me. The disease left me totally paralyzed except for some movement in my right arm and leg. I could not sit up by myself, my whole nervous system was damaged, and most of my muscles did not work. I still could not breathe on my own and needed assistance in breathing, eating, and all other bodily functions. I had been given my cross to bear. My life was completely changed, and I would never be the same again.

PART I

Seek Your Cross

Chapter 1

The Sacrificial Lamb

*"God has one son on earth without sin, but
never one without suffering."*

—St. Augustine of Hippo

The events of March of 1976 changed my life forever,
and yet I don't remember any of it. I was too young,
so I didn't learn anything from it at that time. But it did
begin my life in a way, for it started me down a much different road than others walk—one that Jesus has called me to
travel. Most people receive their vocation at eighteen years
old, not eighteen months old. God was preparing my soul at
a very early age to grow and to live as a handicapped woman
so that I could suffer and, through that suffering, come to
develop a deep and personal relationship with his Son—the
Sacrificial Lamb.

My childhood in the hospital was only just beginning. I
remained in intensive care with no apparent change in my
condition until nine months later. It was the feast day of
St. Bernadette, April 16, 1977, the little girl to whom the

Blessed Mother had appeared in Lourdes, France. A friend of my dad's named Joey flew in from New York and blessed me with his medal of the Virgin Mary. This was the third time he had come to Chicago to pray over me. He put the medal on the left side of my chest and felt his hand get hot. He called Dad over and said, "Hey, Dave, come here! Feel my hand!" Dad told Joey his hand felt hot but didn't think it meant anything. However, Joey insisted in his Brooklyn accent, "Hey, Dave, that's when it's workin'!" Then he moved the medal to the right side of my chest and the temperature of his hand returned to normal. Joey repeated the procedure and one of my lungs began to function. I was able to be taken out of intensive care for the first time since March of 1976, a period of thirteen months.

Beyond the physical sufferings of my handicap, I, like most people, have my fair share of emotional and spiritual sufferings. It would be very easy for me to blame God for this. I certainly didn't do anything at such a young age to deserve this handicap. And so wages a battle within me as the devil tempts me with despair, whispering in my ear, "Jesus gave you your cross; he doesn't love you." But Jesus speaks to me in the depths of my heart or through others. He speaks consoling words and reassures me, saying, "I am right here beside you. You do not need to be afraid. Let me help you. Let us carry your cross together. I have given you a loving family and fulfilled all of your physical needs. What more do you need?"

This is not without a Scriptural basis. As St. Peter puts it, "Cast all your anxieties on him, for he cares about you" (1 Pt 5:7). When my cross seems heavy and burdensome, Jesus says to me, "Come to me, all who labor and are heavy laden, and I will give you rest. Take my yoke upon you and learn from me; for I am gentle and lowly in heart, and you will find rest for your souls. For my yoke is easy and my burden is light" (Mt 11:28–30). Throughout my life, Jesus has taught me about the merits of suffering through the physical limitations and illnesses that I have had to endure.

As I have grown older, and hopefully wiser, I have come to learn that Christ has called me to suffer in a unique way for my salvation, as well as the salvation of others. With that understanding, I have chosen to accept my handicap, knowing that it is a vocation. Like any vocation, it has its highs and lows, but I would not throw away the lows because I would also be throwing away the highs. In my relationship with Christ, I have found that there is joy in the cross because I know there is life after death when we shall see the face of God and feel his infinite love perfectly.

If we look at each individual person, we can see that God has given that person a unique vocation or mission in life. It is a human temptation to try to avoid our vocation and the suffering that may come from it. Suffering can be scary and unappealing if it is not put into a Christian mind frame. We cannot endure it alone, but it attempts to isolate us from others. There is something beautiful hidden in suffering if we look closely enough. There is a small opportunity to triumph over it and turn it into something good. We have the power to transform suffering into sacrifice with our love, just as Jesus did on Calvary. Suffering becomes sacrifice through love. We make a commitment of the will that we will lift our cross amidst all the sufferings that come with it. When we make that commitment and consciously dedicate it for an intention, we reflect the Sacrificial Lamb.

Upon this reflection, we can also come to understand that Jesus made his sacrifice out of love for us and through our suffering; we can participate with him in the salvation of others. Love is sacrificial after all. If we truly love another, we will offer our sacrifices for the good of another, just as Christ did for us. Jesus took on the pains of sin by loving us enough to carry the cross. The Way of the Cross is the story of the ultimate sacrifice; it is also the greatest love story we know. We can elevate our suffering into a sacrificial service to others, but we can only do this consciously and with love for one another. No one can make a sacrifice for themselves; it would violate the very definition of the word. When we dedicate our suffering to others out of love, it becomes something far greater than suffering. It becomes sacrifice, and thus we are able to become united to our Lord on the cross.

Sacrifice is a central theme of our Catholic faith. Not only did our Lord sacrifice himself, but the Mass itself *is* a sacrifice. The central mystery of our faith—the Eucharist—is delivered to us through the sacrifice of the Mass. We enter into a deeper understanding of God's love for us at the Mass, and we partake in his love in a unique and beautiful way as the holy sacrifice is re-presented to us.

Sacrifice is a way for us to show our love for others in the deepest way possible. It is the central facet of our faith because it is the way God reveals his love to us most intimately. When we sacrifice, we are suffering some kind of physical, emotional, psychological, or spiritual pain, sometimes in intense ways. The intensity varies from one person to another, but I think it is safe to say that every human being can be tempted to give up. In suffering, we are made to realize in a very specific way our dependence on God. In a way, we lose the ability to control our lives, and we are forced to realize that we cannot do much for ourselves. Suffering gives us the opportunity to put our trust in God. Whether or not we choose that path is up to each person. Yet sacrifice is a way to imitate Christ's love for others by offering up our crosses as a sacrifice of love for God and petition for others. So sacrifice is the central part of our faith because it can bring us to a deeper understanding of the mystery of Christ's sacrifice on the cross.

Out of all the crosses that we see throughout our life, sometimes it is most difficult to reflect on our own. God has given us all a unique cross to carry. That cross is full of physical pain, emotional angst, and spiritual skepticisms. Yet that cross is individually ours and was made just for us. If we only see it as an unfair weight, we will never gain the spiritual merits from carrying it. Those spiritual merits afford us our own kind of resurrection to heaven. God has taught me that I cannot have the resurrection without the cross.

Chapter 2

The Age-Old Question

*"The real problem is not why some pious, humble,
believing people suffer, but why some do not."*

—C. S. Lewis

Suffering is still largely a mystery to us. If someone has the smallest belief in God and acknowledges his existence, then they ask, "How can a loving God allow good people to suffer?" This same question has been asked through the generations and will continue to be asked. Unfortunately, there is no short cut answer to it—everyone must answer it for themselves. In many cases, a search for this answer brings great spiritual maturity. My own personal search led me to the short answer that suffering is meritorious when it is united to our Lord's suffering on the cross.

In my own life, I can attest to God's love during the most difficult times of suffering, whether it be physical, emotional, or spiritual. I know from family stories the deep anguish and sorrow my parents and siblings felt as they watched me suffer seizures and the pain of all the testing and hospital stays. I know firsthand the daily fear of feeling like I am suffocating from not being able to breathe. I have lived through all the setbacks of hospitalizations due to respiratory failure. As a quadriplegic, the ordinary functions and tasks of daily living are monumental for me, but I want to make myself a witness to others of the power of God's love. I want to show them how that love sustains me throughout my suffering, and how it can sustain them through theirs. I believe that God has invited me to understand in a deeper way the mystery of suffering through the cross of his Son, Jesus.

According to the Latin etymology, the word *suffer* comes from the word *sufferre*, which consists of two words: *sub* and *ferre*—*sub* meaning "under" and *ferre* meaning "to carry or bear." The very nature of the word reflects a burden to bear. The pride we have makes it difficult to be under anything, especially something that weighs on us, something that seemingly hinders us from moving forward, something that prevents us from achieving our worldly successes. Many people find it difficult to accept the reality of suffering. Some ignore it as if it will go away on its own, so long as they don't acknowledge it. Others tremble in its presence and take whatever measures they can to avoid it, as if it were some monster stalking them and a little bit of discomfort is the worst thing imaginable.

Because of this, there is a growing lack of adversity in this world. This does not prepare us for the inevitable pains of life. Tragedy will strike, crisis will come, people we love will die, and we, too, will die one day. We are at a disadvantage in dealing with this, for we are in many respects spoiled by our blessings. And so, when suffering comes, we usually don't know what to do with it. Many people question the very fabric of life and blame God for their woes. They project an air of toughness as they go about their lives, but when they are met with suffering, they get lost very quickly. They no longer know how to navigate life and they refuse to follow their Divine Shepherd. Despair and sorrow weigh too heavily on them and they fold like a house of cards. I've had those same temptations, but most of the time, I can withstand it, for I am constantly exposed to some kind of suffering. It's like an immune system, which grows stronger as it is exposed to more bacteria. Our souls are much like that when they deal with suffering.

So why does God allow us to suffer? Every answer will be unique just as every bit of suffering is unique to a given individual. Just as every person is different from another, so God gives each person a different cross to carry. God chose my cross for me from the day I was born. Neither I nor my parents did anything to cause my sickness. The fact that this cross is mine from the beginning of my life is evidence enough that God has a very special plan for me—one that is very different from most people. Despite the personal nature of our crosses, we can all use them to share in his Son's passion. This was the way he chose to show his love for mankind by redeeming us from sin. I believe this is where we go for the answer. I believe that we find meaning in human suffering when we unite our sufferings to Christ's suffering on the cross.

There is probably not a person in the world who hasn't asked, "How could God allow this to happen?" Perfectly healthy people are stricken with cancer. Loving parents suffer the tragedy of losing a child. Such tragedies naturally beg the question. We may think that it doesn't make sense. We may think that God is cruel for allowing terrible things to happen to good people. But we must recognize suffering for what it is. It is an opportunity to unite our sufferings to Christ's suffering on the cross. We are called to defeat suffering through love, just as Christ Jesus did with his cross. When we are able to do this, we come into a deeper, more intimate friendship with Christ—one that could last for eternity.

CHAPTER 3

The Origin of Suffering

"No one can escape the experience of suffering or the evils in nature which seem to be linked to the limitations proper to creatures: and above all to the question of moral evil."

—*Catechism of the Catholic Church*, no. 385

To best understand how we are allowed to suffer, we must understand origins of suffering. Suffering entered the world with the first man's and woman's sin of pride and disobedience to God. There is a mysterious connection between sin and suffering, one that theologians have explored and one that stems from the Fall. When Adam and Eve sinned, they rejected God's love for them. They did not trust that God loved them, so they listened to the serpent. Adam's decision to deny God's love for them had destructive ramifications. It separated man from God, and with that separation, the long-lasting effects of sin and suffering entered the world.

Let us remember what the serpent said to Eve during the first temptation. "For God knows that when you eat of it your eyes will be opened, and you will be like God, knowing good and evil" (Gn 3:5). After Adam and Eve ate the forbidden fruit, suffering came into the world, and through the effects of original sin, we as a species became discontent with our nature. Something deep within us does not want to admit that we sinned in the garden. There is an internal struggle within each of us between the effects of original sin and the goodness of our soul. We want to be free from this pain—we want to be more than we are. We are embattled with the limits of our nature. Suffering occurs when we meet these limits, whether it be through physical, emotional, or spiritual pain.

I suffer physically every day as my body asserts its strict limitations on me. It is within my nature to walk, to take a deep breath, to lift myself up, but my body rejects those notions and prevents me from doing so. As I am hindered so much by my body, it becomes easier for me to live by the spirit. I have been given a unique opportunity to live a spiritual life because I quite literally can't live a normal physical life. I remember seeing a group of kids play ring around the rosy when I was growing up. I watched from afar and talked to Jesus who was always with me, wherever I went. My body is locked up tight, but my soul is unlocked and wide open for God to fill.

We all should be capable of doing so much more, but evil has taken root and prevents us from doing so, whether that be a physical evil, mental evil, or a spiritual evil. My physical struggle only exhibits what happens in each and every one of us. A struggle between our goodness and our limitations brought about by sin and evil in this world. St.

Augustine tells us in *City of God*, "For evil has no positive nature; but the loss of good has received the name 'evil.'" What this means is that evil is the lack (or privation) of the good. Blindness is a physical evil because it is the lack of sight. Despair is spiritual evil because it is the lack of hope. In a world that is so lacking, how are we to find goodness? Suffering is how we *feel* that lacking. Suffering is how we *feel* evil. We are all confronted with the reality of evil through suffering. It is what we do in the face of this reality that determines its outcome and, in a sense, our outcome.

St. John Paul II delivered a message of suffering in his apostolic letter *Salvifici Doloris*. It gives us a deeper insight into suffering and how it is an inherent part of the human condition when he writes, "It is as deep as man himself, precisely because it manifests in its own way that depth which is proper to man, and in its own way surpasses it. Suffering seems to belong to man's transcendence: it is one of those points in which man is in a certain sense 'destined' to go beyond himself, and he is called to this in a mysterious way.[1]

Suffering is difficult for us to bear because it is an evil being pressed upon a goodness. It pushes us to the ends of human nature and serves as a painful reminder of our limitations. Before the Fall, there was no suffering on this earth, and we were capable of so much more, but suffering originated in the garden as a result of the first sin, and we are contending with the echoes of that rebellion to this day. It was that first sin that necessitated our Savior to come, as the new Adam, and rectify our salvation with his sacrificial love.

---

[1]   *Salvifici Doloris,* no. 2.

As Catholics, we believe when Adam and Eve sinned, they brought suffering into the world, but Christ transformed the act of suffering in his peaceful resignation to the Divine plan. Through his passion, death, and resurrection, Christ was able to transform suffering into sacrifice, which paved the way for man to return to God. Man's offering of his crosses of life become an act of love for God and neighbor that draws us closer together.

CHAPTER 4

Of Different Kinds

*"Jesus permits the spiritual combat as a
purification not as a punishment."*

—St. Pio of Pietrelcina

I have experienced in my life three primary types of suffering: physical, emotional, and spiritual. Although my life
is filled with physical suffering from my handicap, I have
found that this is one of the easiest forms of suffering to
handle.

Much of my life centers around special precautions that I
must take. These are of paramount importance because if I
do not abide by this rigid set of precautions, I could die. For
instance, there is a routine process I contend with called suctioning. Suctioning is where someone inserts a tube down
my stoma (the hole in my neck from my tracheotomy) and
sucks the phlegm out of my chest. I am unable to cough, so
as phlegm naturally builds in my esophagus and my chest,
my ability to breathe diminishes. This is a very painful process that must happen or I will eventually suffocate. Some

days it has to be done over twelve times. Another source of my physical pain is when I sit in my chair for too long, my abdomen begins to hurt because my internal organs are crunching on themselves due to their odd arrangement inside me. Lastly, the scoliosis in my back can be very painful, and with age, it is only getting worse. We fall into a trap when we equate our health to our bodies. We tend to forget that this body of ours is merely a vessel for our passage to the afterlife. It will be discarded at death, until the resurrection of the body when it will rise in its most glorified state.

Emotional pain has also been very difficult for me in the past, as it is for anybody. This form of suffering is much more difficult to cope with than physical suffering. Physical suffering typically doesn't last as long as emotional suffering. Being a quadriplegic, I have been taken care of by someone my entire life. This monumental responsibility was largely handled by my parents and now by my sister. When you are physically helpless for so many things, people can assume that you don't know how to think for yourself. So there have been times when people have thought that I was incapable of thinking on my own, that I was incapable of being mentally, emotionally, or spiritually independent. This caused great strife in my life.

People in our lives will wrong us—that is a certainty. No one goes through life without a strain on a relationship. The closer the relationship, the heavier the burden, but we must remember that forgiveness is the spiritual medicine needed to heal us from emotional suffering. Our Lord showed us this as he hung on his cross. After he had been beaten mercilessly and was left to die before the gathered crowds, including his mother, our Lord still had the ability to say, "Father, forgive them; for they know not what they do" (Lk 23:34). Let us remember that whatever anguish our neighbor puts us through, it is never too much that we can't forgive them. Much like Christ, we should forgive them even if they don't apologize. Their pride may blind them from doing so, but we can forgive deep within our hearts. Only then will the burden of emotional suffering lighten and the wound on our heart begin to close. In order to heal properly, Jesus wants us to pray for the grace of forgiveness, a grace that comes from him alone.

There is a unique type of emotional suffering that, in my opinion, is the hardest to bear. That is when someone we love is suffering. Witnessing this leads us to question God and the problem of pain in a more skeptical way. I think about how my parents and family suffered alongside me as I would go into cardiac arrest or respiratory failure. I will never understand their suffering just as they will never understand mine. Suffering is unique to the person; we all suffer in different ways, and this is part of the problem with someone we know who is suffering—we can't understand. Every empathetic bone in our bodies wants to understand; we want to carry their cross for them, but we can't—because it is theirs.

The single hardest thing I have ever had to do was leaving my parents' care to live with my sister. This was no easy task, and both me and my parents endured a great deal of emotional suffering. I had been under their care for forty years, and although there were reasons to leave, it did not make doing it any easier. I love my parents for what they have done for me all my life, and I recognize how they have suffered alongside me. All of my brothers and sisters have, in some way, suffered alongside me, just as I have suffered alongside them when they met tragedy. It really is a good test of who we love: do we suffer when they suffer? Do we unite ourselves to them in their suffering? We must do that with our Lord, and we must unite ourselves to him and suffer as he suffered. Suffering for another is the greatest proof of love. That is how our Lord showed us his love and how we should show him and others the love we have for them.

I look to Mary when I experience this empathetic kind of suffering. Imagine our Blessed Mother following her Son as he was scourged, as he carried the cross and was nailed to it. She was a witness with Mary Magdalene and the apostle John. Her suffering that day is hard to explain, but in a sense, she, too, had her own passion. When someone we love suffers, whether it be a child, a spouse, a brother, or sister, run to our Lady for help. We must ask her to intercede for us so that we can have the strength that she had on Good Friday. She is our protector as we mourn and weep in this valley of tears. Just as she cradled the Christ child, she, too, can cradle us when we are at our lowest.

Spiritual suffering occurs when we empathize and take on another's spiritual battles or struggles in life to accept their suffering as a gift or something that can be seen as joyful. Everyone experiences spiritual suffering in their own way. I have experienced it by delving into prayer for someone who is struggling and trying to get into their shoes. Sometimes my spiritual suffering is intense because I am lifting them up in prayer and begging the Lord to heal them or at least lighten their burdens. When I pray for someone, I tend to put all of my energy into those prayers because I want what is best for that person according to God's will. I don't know what God's will is for them, and that is what hurts the most.

We can see a great example of spiritual suffering when Jesus suffered in the Garden of Gethsemane. He suffered the enormous burden of the devil tempting him to give up as he saw the torture that was before him. The devil has a way of spiritually dragging me down with his temptations to doubt the love of God and others. He tempts me with the frustration of not being able to do things for myself. This is when I need to place myself in God's hands and accept the cross he has given me. I don't need to be looking for crosses or wanting to be someone that I am not. Spiritual suffering is the battle that I have to fight to overcome these temptations. It is a battle between good and evil. To deny this battle is to deny the truth that we are fallen human beings in need of God's love and mercy. We must remember that this spiritual warfare is constantly waging within each and every one of us and the stakes are higher than any.

CHAPTER 5

Mercy Hospital and the Merciless Doctor

"My God, if my tongue cannot say in every moment that I love you, I want my heart to repeat it as often, as I draw breath."

—St. John Vianney

We all meet suffering at different times, and I am no different. Although I live with a permanent handicap, I, too, get surprised when suffering rears its ugly head. I came face to face with suffering in its rawest form in 1992. Though spinal meningitis struck when I was eighteen months old, I didn't reach the depths of suffering until I was eighteen years old. On November 18, I awoke feeling very tired. That morning I tried to feed myself in my usual manner but found I was too weak to move my arm. I told Mom about my difficulties and she proceeded to feed me herself. However, I was having difficulties breathing and I did not have an appetite. Within minutes, I passed out. From this point, what I write are the memories relayed to me by Mom and Dad while I was in a coma.

Seeing my state of unconsciousness, my mother began to do mouth-to-mouth resuscitation. In between the breaths she blew into me, she screamed at Dad to call 911 for the paramedics. The paramedics arrived and put a tube through my nose to put me on a positive pressure respirator. Then they rushed me to Mercy Hospital in Pittsburgh. Shortly after arriving, I awoke to find myself in the ICU. I looked up at my parents and said, "What am I doing here?" To which they replied, "You passed out; you're in the hospital." I was a very unhappy teenager at that moment. As you can imagine, I have seen many hospital rooms and I did not want to be there. God had other plans for me, though. As we soon discovered, I would have to stay on positive pressure for quite some time. My nose could not take the beating of the large respirator tube and so a second tracheotomy would have to be performed since the first tracheotomy had closed. Hence, I spent many days in the ICU longing for the company of my parents and my brothers and sisters who were living in the Pittsburgh area.

I felt very disheartened when I had to witness on a daily basis the great conflict that occurred between the chief of the ICU and my parents. He actively opposed mine and my parents' wishes to keep the respirator settings at the levels which were most comfortable for me. In his determination to make sure the medical policy of "one remedy fits all" was enforced, he ensured that I was going to be weaned off the respirator no matter if it worked with my body or not—and it didn't work. In his ignorance, he overrode my needs and gave the respiratory therapists orders to gradually decrease the air volume on the respirator. Each time the air was turned down, I would cry because I felt like I was being deliberately suffocated. For instance, one evening when none of my family members were present, one of the respiratory therapists came into my room to carry out the order she was given. Having dozed off to sleep for a few minutes, I awoke to her standing next to my bed turning down the air to my ventilator. I began to mouth the words, "Please don't turn my air down." However, her hands were tied in the matter and she was given no choice but to carry out the doctor's order. I just laid there and cried as the air escaped me. Mom and Dad or one of my brothers would always turn the air up whenever they were visiting, but in these moments of desperation, I cannot tell you how long I had to go before I received the needed amount of air. It happened so frequently during those six weeks that it caused a great struggle between my parents and the chief.

During this time, I complained to my parents that I was being deprived of air. They made sure that if they could not be there to protect me, one of my brothers or sisters in the area would be present. Hence, someone was always in the room to stand guard and make sure the chief did not kill me. Michael, being the good brother that he is, devoted his holiday vacation from the seminary to be my protector and guardian during this trying time. In his efforts, he did a great job of entertaining me with news from home. He and Joe convinced Dad to get a camcorder so they could make home videos of family members who visited during the Christmas holidays and share them with me as I lay in a hospital bed bored to tears.

While my body was under stress in fighting pneumonia, I had the added emotional stress of fighting a spiritual battle of whether to fight to live or to give up and die. When I consciously made an effort to trust in God, it became clear that he was right there at my side sustaining me with his grace. His grace was a gift of courage to continue to persevere amidst the physical and emotional suffering. As I have reflected on these years, it has become apparent to me that I was suffering the difficulties of society's disrespect for human life. As a Catholic Christian, I leaned heavily on my faith and the teachings of the Church to love as Christ loves. I tried to see the chief as a child of God and love him despite the fact he was my enemy.

I realized that the chief held my life in his hands; likewise, he was aware of the great power he had over me. I was scared that he would kill me, and I remember many times praying to Jesus and Mary directly to guide me through this suffering. This time of relentless emotional pain in turn became a time for spiritual growth. Each day, I tried to make my suffering an offering to God by uniting it with him on the cross in an effort to draw closer to him. In that time of suffering, I became intensely aware that God was truly with me. Jesus became my friend and companion. As the offering of my suffering became a habitual practice, it became a subconscious or routine act of the will.

Since I thought at times that I was alone in my suffering, my imagination went wild and I began to wonder if I was going to die. I would talk to the Lord and say, "What do you want of me?" I usually have difficulty waiting for an answer when it does not come immediately. Occasionally, I would continue a conversation without waiting for a reply. As I lay in bed, I continued the dialogue: "If you want me, you can take me. Otherwise, give me the strength to persevere. I'm emotionally exhausted and discouraged. On my own, I cannot fight any more. I need your grace."

He heard my prayers and gave me the strength for that moment. This is usually how God would answer my prayers—one minute at a time. Jesus taught me to depend on his loving providential care, and in those particular moments of suffering, I felt that he said to me, "Therese, I gave you your life and I am the One who will sustain it. You just need to believe in my love for you." I also recited Mother Teresa's prayer over and over again: "Jesus in my heart, I believe in your tender love for me. I love you." This prayer is so practical for our daily spiritual growth in the Lord. I like this prayer because, when I say it, I am accepting Jesus's love for me and I am giving the gift of my love back to him.

On one particular day, the power of prayer was revealed to me in a unique way. I awoke from a nap to the sound of my parents, Kathy, her husband and children, and Fr. Peter all praying the Rosary together in the next room. The experience was so real that I could hardly wait to tell Mom about it when she came in. When she came to visit me, I asked her, mouthing the words, "Are Kathy and her husband here with the kids? Is Fr. Peter here? I heard you guys praying the Rosary together for me."

She looked at me with a puzzled look that said, "Are you crazy?"

I said, "I really heard you praying the Rosary in the next room. Were you all here praying the Rosary?"

Again, she said, "No." This time she looked as though she believed me and did not question my authenticity. She treated it as a situation where God was trying to console me, knowing this was a period of great suffering for me. Maybe it was a vision, maybe it was a hallucination from the extreme toll my body had undergone, but whatever it was, God gave it to me as a comfort in that dark, lonely time.

When we take time to reflect on the past, it can be painful, and so we avoid any occasions to examine our consciences regarding these difficult times. Upon a deeper reflection, God bestowed on me an incredible amount of grace to persevere through my time at Mercy Hospital to keep my faith in him ever alive.

Mercy Hospital and the loneliness that I contended with there marks a period in my life where I met the face of suffering. I look back on that time and think of how terrible it was, but I also think to myself that it was where my individual relationship with God started. I became resigned to the fact that I could die, and so it brought about intimate conversations with God and gritty battles with the devil. This time laid the foundation for my spiritual life, and I can't be anything but thankful to God for giving me that cross, which brought me closer to him.

Chapter 6

Fear and Loneliness

"I still think that the greatest suffering is being lonely,
feeling unloved, just having no one. . . . That is the worst
disease that any human being can ever experience."

—St. Teresa of Calcutta

One time, back when I was only five years old, on a beautiful Sunday morning in August, my family was awakened by the frantic sounds of a whistle. But it wasn't just any whistle; it was the whistle Dad had given the nurse who cared for me at my house. The sound of it signaled an emergency. Rushing up to my room, my parents found that the respirator had malfunctioned and was stuck in the inhale position. As a result, it had blown a hole in both my lungs, collapsing them and filling me with so much air that my face, head, and body looked like a balloon. The nurse had disconnected the respirator and attempted to pump air into my lungs by hand. She was simultaneously giving me CPR because my heart had stopped. Dad immediately called the paramedics. Mom started hand-pumping air into me while the nurse continued her efforts with CPR.

The paramedics arrived in less than three minutes and rushed me back to Children's Memorial Hospital in Chicago. By inserting very long, thin needles into me, doctors were able to remove most of the excess air that had ravaged my body. I remained at Children's Memorial Hospital for about a week before they could send me home. I had been saved again. Over the next two years, my diaphragm strength gradually improved until I was able to remain off the ventilator most of the time.

One time when my mother came to visit me at Children's Memorial Hospital, she asked me, "What do you do when we are not here, Therese?" I answered, "I play peek-a-boo with baby Jesus." This younger version of myself had a playful innocence that helped me through those difficult times. The issue at that time was fear. There were many doctors and machines; to a two-year-old, that can be scary. But as I grew older, the fear faded a bit and a new adversary showed itself: loneliness.

Just as in every human life, there are peaks and valleys of the spiritual life. So too, later in life, while I was at Mercy Hospital as an eighteen-year-old, there were peaks and valleys. The consolation of God's love was often darkened by fear and doubt. The devil tempted me to reject God's love by making me think that all of the suffering I was experiencing was a result of God forgetting about me or not caring for me. The serpent wanted me to feel that I was all alone in the moments of my emotional pain and suffering. In truth, I was anything but. My parents, brothers, sisters, extended family, and friends all came to visit me and prayed for me relentlessly. Even still, I had to consciously fight against feelings of despair and despondence. It was so important for me to feel surrounded by the love of those who were close to me. Their love and support were like spiritual ammunition to overcome the temptations of the devil. We need this as we go through times of pain and suffering, for it is impossible to carry the heavy burdens of pain alone. We need to be able to share the experiences of our suffering with others. Even in Christ's own passion, Simon of Cyrene was there to share the weight of the cross with him. Asking for help may be the hardest thing to do in that time, but it is the most critical.

Suffering attempts to isolate us. Oftentimes, we will withdraw from others in response to suffering and ask ourselves questions like, "How could anyone ever understand how I feel, especially if I can't even put into words just how I feel?" Because suffering is such an internalized thing, whether it be in our bones, heart, or soul, it is in a sense an individual experience. We know our cross is ours and ours alone, specifically designed for us, like a spiritual fingerprint—no two are alike. Let us not forget what our Lord said as he hung on his cross: "And about the ninth hour Jesus cried with a loud voice, 'Eli, Eli, la'ma sabach-tha'ni?' that is, 'My God, my God, why hast thou forsaken me?'" (Mt 27:46). Even our Lord felt that loneliness and directed his questions to God the Father. It's okay for us to do the same.

During this dark time of loneliness at Mercy Hospital, I was tempted to despair. I was no longer the two-year-old playing peek-a-boo with Jesus. I was an independent thinking adult who began asking questions. I watched people check in to the adjacent room and check out under a sheet. I would see it and say, "Am I going to be next? If it is, okay." In my experience, there is a disconnect between the spiritual and physical aspects of life. I tended to have thoughts of the spiritual rather than the physical realm of life, as my physical abilities were more limited than others. I began to think of death as merely a passage from this life to eternal life; this would become a momentous step in my spiritual life as it instilled in me the proper perspective to live by. I would eventually be released; the doctors sent us home and told us that they believed I was going to die in a week. That was twenty-seven years ago. I guess we had the last laugh, after all, and I could only laugh because when I got home, I hopped in my porta-lung and got all the air I needed to do so!

Mercy Hospital was a very difficult time for me, but I took something with me from that awful place. I brought a friend, someone who I could talk to when I was alone or wanted to be alone, someone who would comfort me in the many years to come as I grappled with the struggles of handicapped life. I could feel my physical life draining at Mercy Hospital; I felt it could slip away from my grasp at any moment. But I was able to establish a grip on my personal relationship with Christ, and from that day forward, I swore I would never let go.

CHAPTER 7

How to Find Our Cross

"There is no better wood for feeding the fire of
God's love than the wood of the cross."

—St. Ignatius of Loyola

We meet our crosses in different ways. Sometimes they are unexpectedly given to us, like it was to me, while other times a period of natural discernment occurs. As we heed God's calling and follow his will, we find our cross to bear in life. It may be the married life, it may be the religious life, or it may be the single life, like in my case. I am referring, of course, to our vocation. Our vocation can lead us to our suffering and give it purpose in this life. We must stop and listen to what God is calling us to do. This is easier for some and more difficult for others. We must keep in mind that when we are discerning, we are really asking ourselves for whom we are meant to suffer. Maybe we are destined to suffer for a spouse and our children, or maybe a flock if you are to become a parish priest. In my case, I am a consecrated single, so I am destined to suffer for Christ. I see this as the greatest honor of my life. Once we find our vocation, we must live it each and every day, dedicated to the Mystical Body of Christ, for it is how we serve him. This vocation is the cross we must bear through life. If we bear it only for ourselves, we will fall under its weight. If we bear it for someone else, the love of that sacrifice will be the strength we need to carry it.

I recall a wise priest once saying in a homily, "To bring suffering upon ourselves is not an authentic act of sacrifice. It is foolishness. The authentic sacrifice is accepting the crosses that God gives to us. There is humility and a holy docility in accepting the crosses God gives us instead of willfully bringing suffering upon ourselves." Suffering for ourselves can never be sacrifice.

My vocation as a consecrated single woman is a little bit different than most single women because God has called me to be a bold witness to the joy in the cross. Everybody has suffering, but it is our outlook on suffering that will define who we are. I believe that my mission as a single woman is to show through my actions and words that I can be joyful in the midst of suffering. It is an attitude that I have chosen when I don't feel like expressing joy. Sometimes I don't feel joyful with myself, but with God's help, I don't have too much trouble finding something positive about my suffering. This is the case particularly when I have people lifting me up and helping me to see the goodness of God in my cross.

It is okay that we might battle with this calling. That's only natural. We have our own plans and it is hard to remember that God has his own plans for us. Even Mary, our Mother, when Gabriel came to her at the Annunciation, asked the angel:

> And Mary said to the angel, "How can this be, since I have no husband?" And the angel said to her,
>
> "The Holy Spirit will come upon you, and the power of the Most High will overshadow you; therefore the child to be born will be called holy, the Son of God.
>
> And behold, your kinswoman Elizabeth in her old age has also conceived a son; and this is the sixth month with her who was called barren. For with God nothing will be impossible." And Mary said, "Behold, I am the handmaid of the Lord; let it be to me according to your word." And the angel departed from her. (Lk 1:34–38)

This passage shows us a tremendous amount of insight. First, notice how much Mary speaks versus how much she listens. Secondly, our vocation, much like our cross, typically doesn't make sense immediately. The question of why is not always answered. That is why we must love our cross. It is an act of the will, not an exercising of logic. We must be fully committed to something we don't fully understand. God does not expect us to give a mediocre or indifferent response to the vocation to which he has called us. Rather, he has called us to say a complete yes to his will, just as Mary said yes in accepting the cross of bearing Jesus and giving him to the world.

Most likely an angel won't appear out of the sky to explain what God has in store for us. So how do we find our vocation? Each person finds their vocation in their own way. I found my vocation by making a habit throughout my life of spending quiet moments with the Lord in prayer. It is very important that we spend time conversing with the Lord. It can surely be hard to set aside that time though, so let us remember Matthew 6:6, "But when you pray, go into your room and shut the door and pray to your Father who is in secret; and your Father who sees in secret will reward you" (Mt 6:6). Why should we shut our door to pray? Privacy. We need to block out all of the distractions our world shows us and have meaningful conversations with God. Only then can we ever expect to hear his calling. Only then can we answer his calling.

Almost every day, I go on a "walk." Of course, it's not really a walk; it is a ride in my electric wheelchair. This is my favorite part of my day for a number of reasons. First of all, it is the *only* time I am alone. Sometimes my friends ask me, "What do others take for granted?" My answers are typically obvious—walking, feeding yourself, breathing with no difficulty, typing . . . pretty much anything. But one thing that isn't obvious is privacy. As a quadriplegic, I am almost never alone. Someone is taking care of me all day long. If they aren't in the same room as me, they are in the next room listening for me. Not on my walks though. Each day, I have an hour to myself when I am able to navigate my beautiful neighborhood. Behind my house is a lake with bridges and all kinds of ducks and birds. This is where I meet God—in his creation. This private moment is critical for me and, in many respects, is the most important part of my day because it is where I have the deepest dialogue with God. Most people just use prayer as a venting session where they list their demands to God. While supplication is a form of prayer, prayer with God is supposed to be a dialogue, not a monologue.

When we have a dialogue, it requires us to listen. It is a back and forth. A real friendship is rooted in real conversation, and real conversations don't happen over a movie or video games; they happen among privacy and silence. It is hard to listen these days because of all the distractions of technology. Music is constantly playing and videos are constantly streaming—it's scary how plugged in most people are. This is where the first sacrifice must take place. Remember, sacrifice doesn't have to be something huge. Start by setting aside time. That in and of itself is a small sacrifice. It's not always easy, but it is critical that we sacrifice parts of our busy world for privacy and dialogue with God. Maybe we take a walk, maybe we find ourselves in adoration or with our family in our living room saying a Rosary together. Whatever it is, this time must be sacred to our schedule. We must find that time not only to speak to God but also to listen to him. In that time of holy meditation, we will be able to hear God's calling. Maybe not immediately, but eventually his plan will become clear and begin to take shape. What shape does it take? It takes the shape of a cross—our cross. God tells us what crosses we are meant to carry; we just have to listen and respond by accepting, lifting, and carrying it.

Prayer for Seeking Your Cross

Jesus, you have willed that I meet this physical, emotional, and spiritual pain as part of your providential plan. I am hurting, Lord. Give me the grace to acknowledge my suffering and to put you at the center of my life as I endure this cross which you are allowing me to carry for my own salvation and the salvation of others. I need you! I cannot carry this cross on my own. It is much too heavy for me. Please, come and dwell with me now! Take this cross; carry it with me and for me, for without you, I will drop it. Help me to love my cross just as you loved yours on Calvary. You loved us with every fiber of your being, so much so that you were willing to suffer the cruel torture of crucifixion. Help me to love others like you did. I don't have the ability to love like you. Left to my own sinful humanity, I would drop the cross in an instant, but with you, I find my strength, joy, and peace. With you, I can find some relief in the pain I suffer because I know that suffering is not in vain when you are at the center of my life. Amen.

PART II

Embrace Your Cross

CHAPTER 8

Trusting In God

"A humble soul does not trust itself, but
places all its confidence in God."

—St. Faustina

Most people today go to great extents to be in control of everything. We can have *what* we want *when* we want it at the touch of a button. We are conditioned to be the rulers of our reality. We feel like we can plot out our entire lives, but in reality, God may have different plans for us. The one painful yet honest reminder of that fact is suffering. Men and women avoid it at all costs because people do not like being reminded of their own limitations. Being cognizant of our limitations is imperative to embrace for our salvation. How can we live in accordance with God's will if we don't recognize that it truly is in control and to trust in it completely?

As we hear God's calling, we must then embrace the cross he has in store for us. This is a very difficult thing for us because it is the cross God desires us to bear, and sometimes it is not the one we would have chosen for ourselves. Circumstances most likely will not align for our life's perfect plan to become a reality, so we must be adaptable and trusting. "Trust in the LORD with all your heart, and do not rely on your own insight. In all your ways acknowledge him, and he will make straight your paths" (Prv 3:5–6). We must take solace in the knowledge that God knows what will yield our ultimate happiness and what is the best life for us to live. He gives us all the opportunity to live that life through the gift of our crosses.

People try to pick and choose their sacrifices—maybe a father stays late at work to work a little harder, maybe an athlete works a little harder in the gym. These sacrifices are willingly accepted and rewarded when the father gets a promotion and the athlete gets a scholarship. These are temporal rewards, which are easier to aspire toward. Even something as simple as a diet to lose weight. There is a proximate and visible reward waiting for them, like when someone sees they have lost ten pounds. Sometimes God's will does not align with our wishes and the benefits of our crosses aren't immediately recognizable. Spiritual rewards are less tangible and sometimes harder to feel, but we must trust God that it is what we *need* even if it is not what we *want*. I see this very clearly when I look at my handicap. No one would ever wish to have spinal meningitis, and I don't blame anyone. God willed it so, and so I know that there must be a plan for me. I must embrace this cross, for we did not gain the joy of the Resurrection until Jesus bore the weight of the cross upon his shoulders.

God loves us no matter how fallen we are, and his love will carry us through the most difficult times. Trust in God is telling God that I place myself in his hands and I believe that he will bring about the greatest good in the worst of times. Saint Therese is a wonderful example of the child-like trust we should all have. She calls it abandonment to the Will of God. She believed there was no better place to be than in his arms. I try to practice her humility by saying, "I do not have the answers, Lord, but you do." I have been afraid on many occasions, but I continue to learn that true love for our Lord casts out all fears. Saint Teresa of Calcutta was another courageous woman who put her trust in the Lord while she continued her service to the poorest of the poor. She accepted everything as a gift from God, both the good things of life and the hardships. This acceptance is shown through my favorite prayer, the one I have said countless times throughout my life, "I take what you give and I give what you take." Everything I have experienced in my life has been a gift from the Lord, both the good and the bad. My suffering has been difficult, but when I am able to put my full childlike trust in God, that same suffering has led me into a deeper relationship with Jesus, and I thank him for that.

When I put my faith in God and realize that he is in control, it naturally makes me want to know him more. He has all of my love, yet I don't fully understand his calling from time to time. This breeds only a deeper desire for him. We see this with the people that we love; maybe it is why opposites attract so well. When we love someone, yet we don't understand where they are coming from or how they are thinking, we try to get inside their brain to understand. This is an impossible task, like when a man tries to understand his wife (that will never happen) or when we try to understand God. God is a mystery—three persons in one God. His essence transcends logic, so we can't understand it like some complex algebra problem. That doesn't mean that we can't try though. In fact, we all are trying in our own ways, whether it be through the Mass or service to others or studies.

My earliest memory of trusting in God came when I was five years old. My parents wanted me to try a negative pressure respirator, better known as "the iron lung," because they were told it would be safer and healthier for me. We had to travel from Greenwich, Connecticut to a hospital in Augusta, Georgia to test out the iron lung. Hospitals scared me, and so the fear began to set in. They put me in the iron lung, which was gigantic. It weighed eight hundred pounds and it was very long and very wide. I thought it was going to swallow me whole. We called it "the Yellow Submarine," and to get in it, we had to pull out a bed tray for me to lay on. Then someone had to push my head through a porthole and fasten a plastic collar around my neck which sealed the machine from leaking air. After that, someone pushed the bed tray back in and clamped these levers down on the side to lock the iron lung in place. This was a very scary process for someone as young as I was who had never been in such an environment. Then they turned the motor on and the machine breathed for me. To a five-year-old, it was powerful, and I had to learn to subconsciously breathe with the rhythm of the iron lung. Yet I was in no mind frame to consider this new possibility. My fear cut my breaths short. Several doctors and nurses dressed in white uniforms stood there staring at me and making their medical observations. I began to cry; it was all very overwhelming to me. I was afraid, and all I wanted to do was escape. Dad saw this and asked the doctors and nurses to leave in order to have a private conversation with me. He convinced me to pretend I liked the iron lung for the doctors' sakes so that they would be satisfied enough to let me leave the hospital. Right then, I had to trust my earthly father to know what was best for me because I was not sure. God the Father wanted me to trust him and open up my mind to the new possibility of the iron lung. In his wisdom, God the Father and the Holy Spirit knew that this would be a life changing experience for both me and my family. It made caregiving much easier for them because the iron lung is non-invasive and didn't take much care. Positive pressure required twenty-four hour nursing care because it involved respirator tubes needing sterilization every day and there was the endless possibility of me coming down with a respiratory infection. The iron lung allowed us to live independent lives and spend more time with each other as a family. Even with all the fear I felt, I was able to put my trust in both my heavenly Father and my earthly father and show the doctors the results they needed to see. This exercise in trust proved to be a life changing moment, for I would not have been able to be who I am today without it.

Through my journey with spinal meningitis, I learned to trust in God every day of my life, especially in moments when I felt like giving up. The need for trust seemed the most intense when I had a cold and my lungs would fill up with phlegm. In those days, I had some strength in my lungs to cough, but I needed my family to give me that extra boost when the mucus was too thick to bring up. A certain amount of panic would set in if I couldn't breathe. My lungs would get so hard that I couldn't get a breath in and it felt like I was suffocating. I needed to be around someone all the time when I had a cold for fear that I would pass out. Everybody in my family knew how to help me—even my Down syndrome brother, Paul, became an expert at helping me to cough. To help me cough, my family members would do bronchial drainage, which consisted of cupping their hands and patting me on my chest to loosen the mucus lodged in my lungs. Then they would gently push upwards underneath my rib cage and that allowed me to blow the mucus out through my trach since blowing my nose was impossible. I had to trust that God, with the help of my family members, would give me the courage and physical strength to find relief in breathing in those moments. If I allowed panic and fear to consume me, then I could not focus on getting better or finding relief for my lungs. Trusting in God gave me the peace and joy I needed to survive this suffering. Trust begets love and love casts out all fear. Even as a child, I became accustomed to placing my life in God's hands, and I learned to believe that he would sustain my life even when I thought my life could slip away.

CHAPTER 9

A Mother's Touch

*"The Son of God became man for our salvation
but only in Mary and through Mary."*

—St. Louis Marie de Montfort

M ary provides us with a perfect example of having
faith in God. When she was approached by the angel
Gabriel and she was told that she would be the Mother of
God and that the power of the Most High would overshadow
her. How could she respond with anything other than trust
in God? A virgin birth would be a miracle—it was impossible; it bent logic until it broke—but Mary responded how a
loving servant would, "Behold, I am the servant of the Lord;
let it be to me according to your word." Notice that she
didn't say, "I understand and I accept," because she didn't
have to understand it. Just as we don't have to completely
understand our crosses to accept them.

Mary accepted her vocation, and with it came suffering.
Tradition tells us she was only fifteen. Her husband-to-be
left her (eventually to return), she traveled across the desert

pregnant, and she gave birth in a stable among the dirt and the animals. I can't imagine any fifteen-year-old going through that today. Imagine her pain and her worry as the innkeeper shut them out. Imagine how cold it must have been and how many women died during childbirth back then. The birth of Christ was not some shiny event like our nativity sets show us. There were no kings and queens around; there were no extended family present or royal visitors. It was cold, dirty, and lonely. There was a great deal of suffering that night, but it was in this time that the Christ child was born. In the Bible, we literally meet Jesus for the first time within the context of extreme suffering. This is a reminder to us that we too can meet Christ in our suffering.

The origin of suffering, as previously discussed, was the first sin, when Adam and Eve committed the sin of pride by disobeying God with the fruit in hand. The Church tells us that Mary is the new Eve. Jesus is the new Adam. Together, they suffered, and with love, they transformed that suffering into sacrifice. Mary sacrificed for her Son and her Son sacrificed for us. Mary can help us conquer our suffering by being the example needed for bringing our pain to our Lord. Many statues depict Mary with a snake under her sandal, depicting her triumphant victory over the devil. Simply put, evil is allergic to Mary. Even in modern exorcisms, it is said that invoking Mary's name is especially effective in rooting out the demons inside.

What is so beautiful about Mary is that she is human and was born without original sin, yet she still suffered in a world full of evil. Despite her own flawless nature, she still had to live in a flawed world—one that would eventually murder her only Son. How did she handle herself through this? With serenity. Let us petition for this beautiful virtue in our sufferings through the Serenity Prayer: Lord, grant me the serenity to accept the things I cannot change, the courage to change the things I can, and the wisdom to know the difference.

Everyone is eventually met with suffering that they didn't invoke themselves. This kind of suffering is the hardest to face for we feel unprepared for it. Always remember, though, that Mary must have felt incredibly unprepared to carry the Son of God, but God had prepared her with a flawless soul, untainted by original sin. God has also prepared us for the crosses we meet. We might not understand how, but Mary and the saints remind us of what we as humans can endure. Despite the effects of original sin, God has given us a beautiful soul equipped with an intellect and a will to diffuse the evil of suffering and to turn it into sacrifice with love.

Mary is the perfect model of one who surrenders to our Lord. We can say with her, "O Jesus, I surrender myself to you, take care of everything!" (Fr. Don Dolindo). So many events in her life were above her understanding. Imagine raising and parenting a child who is omniscient! Despite the angel Gabriel and the Annunciation, Jesus's mission on earth must have been slowly revealed to our Lady. She couldn't understand why he left her to go teach in the temple. She couldn't understand why he had to die. She couldn't understand the fullness of Jesus's ministry, but she did incite it. Remember that it was Mary who nudged our Lord and urged him to perform his first miracle at the wedding feast at Cana. Despite her lack of understanding, she trusted fully in God's Will and not only watched it in action but became a powerful instrument of it by bringing our Savior to us.

The greatest example we see of her steadfast fidelity to Jesus was when she stood at the foot of the cross. St. John Paul II speaks of Mary's faith and love when he writes:

> At the foot of the Cross Mary shares through faith in the shocking mystery of this self-emptying. This is perhaps the deepest 'kenosis' of faith in human history. Through faith the Mother shares in the death of her Son, in his redeeming death; but in contrast with the faith of the disciples who fled, hers was far more enlightened. On Golgotha, Jesus through the Cross definitively confirmed that he was the 'sign of contradiction' foretold by Simeon. At the same time, there were also fulfilled on Golgotha the words which Simeon had addressed to Mary: 'and a sword will pierce through your own soul also.'[2]

Along with Jesus, Mary suffered the excruciating pain of the evil of suffering. Mary confronted the brutality and cruelty embodied in moral evil and she stood faithfully with her Son as he endured his passion. How could any of this make sense at the time? They were viciously murdering her Son who had committed no wrong, then or at any time in his life. She is the ultimate witness to suffering as she witnessed

2   John Paul II, *Redemptoris Mater:* On the Blessed Virgin Mary in the Life of the Pilgrim Church (Liberia Editrice Vaticana, 1987), accessed March 17, 2017, http://w2.vatican.va/content/ john-paul-ii/en/encyclicals/documents/hf_jp-ii_enc_25031987_ redemptoris-mater.html.

the greatest sacrifice in human history. Jesus had to die to right the wrongs of Adam and all those who followed. Jesus had to take on the sins of the world and transform suffering into sacrifice. At the foot of the cross, Mary had to trust God that this had to be done, even though it was outside of her understanding. We can turn to her when we are in need, especially when we have to put our trust in the Lord. She serves as the greatest vehicle of prayer to our Lord. Just as a child runs to their mother when they are hurt, let us run to our Lady who will comfort us as the loving mother she is. "To thee do we cry, poor banished children of Eve. To thee do we send up our sighs, mourning and weeping in this valley of tears!"

CHAPTER 10

The Body and the Brain

*"Tribulation is a gift from God—one that he
especially gives to His special friends."*

—St. Thomas More

My brother Paul has Down syndrome and is fifteen months older than me. I consider it a great blessing to be his little sister. He was an adorable toddler with his typical Down syndrome traits: small head and facial features, somewhat squinty eyes, and tiny box-like little teeth that were almost perpetually being displayed in his constant smile. He was very mild-mannered and extremely affectionate, exhibiting his devotion by frequently planting his trademarked sloppy kisses on my cheek. His tongue was an overwhelming presence in this act. It seemed as though I was being attacked by his love, and I would yell in protest each time I perceived the approaching bestowal of a Paul kiss. His sense of style was as pronounced as his kisses; he capitalized on the straightness of his thick blonde hair by combing it directly forward into his eyes, a fashion our brothers tried to remedy as he got older, using gel in an attempt to sweep it to the side.

We are very close, and we used to get in all sorts of trouble together as toddlers. Being so inseparable, there was a lot of arguing and nitpicking that went on between the two of us that still exists today. Mom recalls how, fearing his slobbery kisses above all else, I would be on constant lookout for my big brother. Even from the other end of the hall, I would start to scream if I saw Paul coming, thinking that the noise would have an effect on him or alert Mom so she would tell him to leave me alone. Paul was a very stubborn boy, especially in the things that he expressly *didn't* want to do. Since it is very difficult to reason with someone with Down syndrome, it was nearly impossible to shake him out of these strong-willed moments. Once, not keen on the idea of a walk down the street, he plopped himself down in the middle of the road. Nothing Mom would say could entice him to budge. In order to finish her stroll, she had to carry him.

Despite our quarrels, Paul and I played very well together. One time, we got the vacuum hose and spoke into each end like a telephone. Paul would shout into his end of the hose while I listened on the other end; then I would shout into it while he listened on his end. To this day, he loves to take out the picture of us and our vacuum telephone game, recalling the story of that moment as we have heard it from our older siblings. Likewise, he will produce a second picture in which we are sitting side by side on the couch dressed up as king and queen, relating the story as if he remembers it himself. Yet another favorite picture of Paul and me, depicts us in our respective high chairs, covered in food. Apparently, we had even turned eating into a game. One day, when Mom put Paul and me down for a nap, my innovative brother decided that the potted plants between our beds would look much better inside the bed. He got up and promptly dumped one plant into his bed and another into mine. The next part of his plan was to climb in bed with me and my new decoration. Not long after, Mom checked on us and found us covered in black dirt, sound asleep. She surveyed the mess and simply retreated, quietly closing the door so as not to disturb our nap.

Paul has been and continues to be a major part of my life. He is my closest sibling, and he is a source of love to all his family, especially me. My brother may not be very smart in most people's eyes, but he has taught me the greatest lesson that one can ever learn, and that is how to love.

Paul is a living example of the joy and the sadness of the cross. In his very nature, he is happy, loving, kind, and trusting. With his mental handicap, Paul suffers from the lack of being able to communicate his thoughts and feelings clearly to others. It takes a special person to understand these feelings Paul cannot express and an acute sensitivity for Paul's needs and desires. I do not think I can say that I have always had this ability, but I have tried to understand him. One of the ways I show my sensitivity toward him is to try to compensate for his inability to express himself. If I saw that someone did not understand what Paul was saying, I made a point of translating or interpreting for him. As our relationship matured to adulthood, I have come to understand his suffering a *little* better. I can never fully understand what he suffers, though, because I am not him.

Paul and I relied strongly on each other, where he was my "muscle man" and I was his "brain." Whenever he wanted to write something, he would ask me to spell words for him. I, in turn, expected him to drop everything and move me from one location to the other. In this way, we complemented each other. He could depend on me mentally, while I could depend on him physically. This yielded a great friendship for, as two handicapped people, we were not depended on much by others.

There is one profoundly fundamental teaching of the Church that my family in particular has embraced, and that is fighting for the preservation of the dignity of life at every phase of life. The most obvious cause for the pro-life movement is saving unborn babies from being deprived of the life to which God has called them. Yet the pro-life cause does not end with the unborn. It is seen in the disrespect for the handicapped and the elderly who are considered "worthless" to society because our culture measures a person based on their productivity in society. In my belief that God has a vocation for each of us, I want to say that Paul's vocation started at the moment of his conception. Back in the '70s, there were no sonograms, so my parents did not find out that Paul was special until his birth. The moment after his birth, the doctors pressured Mom to put Paul in an institution because society encouraged parents with special needs children to put them away so they would not be seen. Mom and Dad said, "No. We are going to keep him and raise him just like we have raised our thirteen other normal children." The doctors said, "How can you do this?" And Mom answered, "What do you mean? I am going to love him." Knowing Mom, she probably thought, "This is what you do for a child. Why would raising a Downs like Paul be any different?" This once again evinces the loving strength both of my parents have had. If it wasn't difficult enough to take care of Paul growing up, I came along and contracted the disease, adding to the daily workload. But they did not blink and did exactly what they told the doctor they were going to do—they loved us.

Paul and I were clearly given our vocations of suffering with handicaps from the moment of our conception. However, my vocation did not manifest itself until after my birth. I take comfort in the fact that God gave me Paul as a silent voice of support in living out the call to be a witness to life through my handicap. Through his manifestation of love for me, Paul has been a tremendous support to me in continuing to love when all seems hopeless. Faced with a severely harsh disease, there are times when I am tempted to give up. Then I reach out to Paul and he gives me one of his trademarked sloppy kisses or an infectious smile. His joy permeates each environment he enters, and he has a way of giving such reassurance that everything will be okay. After that, I have to say to myself, "Snap out of it, Therese! Stop feeling sorry for yourself. There are others that suffer more than you." Paul may not realize the trials of being mentally handicapped, but that doesn't mean he doesn't feel its effects.

Paul has had an incredible impact on me because he is the only person who has ever needed me as much as I needed him (at least physically). I was his brain and he was my body.

We grew up together and my parents sacrificed everything for us. Leaving them and him was the most difficult thing I would ever do. We were quite the duo, and I love when he comes to visit me so we can celebrate the 'nationally mandated holiday' of his birthday. This celebration continues throughout the year and repeats itself four or five times. The fact that he celebrates so many birthdays reminds me of how his mind is younger than ours and has retained its childlike innocence. A pure, untainted joy lives there—one that I aspire to have for myself. I see that mirth living inside him and I know it still drives him in every thought, in every birthday party, and in every sloppy kiss.

CHAPTER 11

The Humor of It All

*"There was some one thing that was too great for God
to show us when He walked upon our earth; and I
have sometimes fancied that it was His mirth."*

—G. K. Chesterton

One of the best ways I have found to accept my cross is to have a sense of humor and to laugh at myself when I find the burdens too difficult to bear. I learned this very difficult lesson largely from each of my brothers and sisters in a different way. My mom also played a major role in developing this light-hearted outlook that I carry with me. This is one of the benefits of a large family—they kept me in check and never allowed me to feel sorry for myself. This ability to laugh at myself helps me to see the positive in a negative situation. In many ways, I laugh things off that are really serious. It is kind of the Irish way to find humor in really hurtful situations so that I don't dwell too much on how intensely I am hurting.

I remember one time in particular when most of us were in our big family van and we were driving down the street. All of a sudden, my sisters and I saw our brother driving by; he began waving at us and pointing at our van. We stopped and realized that the engine was smoking. Someone yelled, "It's going to blow!" and so everyone screamed and ran out of the van. They all gathered behind the van and realized shortly that they had left their handicapped sister, Therese, in the van. Fortunately for me, the van did not explode and we now can look back on that story with a good laugh.

I remember my brother, Father Peter, saying once that laughter is the best healing remedy. He said there have been studies on people who have made a point of laughing with others when they have a chronic illness. Their ability to laugh helps relieve the awful symptoms of their illness. I think that's really true because I know that when I was sick and certain siblings came to visit me, they would make a point of finding humor in the little things, and this ability to laugh would help me to get better.

It is hard yet very important to keep a positive attitude and find the joy in the little things of life even when I am suffering a lot. In a sense, when you have a sense of humor towards life, there is a certain amount of happiness, joy, and peace that comes from being able to laugh. A smile goes a long way. Sometimes I don't feel like smiling, but when I am with others, I do it in spite of myself or how I feel at that moment. My feelings come and go just like any other person's. Though I have strong feelings, I try to keep them in check. I have an attitude that says "no one likes a grouch," so when I have to depend on others for help, I try to be kind and happy. It is the same when I meet new people. I always try to smile and be happy and enthusiastic about life.

One night while I was in my porta-lung, I woke up to a June bug crawling on my pillow next to my face. I looked at it and then I started calling for Michael who slept in the adjacent room and listened for me. I didn't want to scare him too much, so I called softly at first, but as the bug crawled closer to my face, I started calling more loudly. When Michael came in, pure dread came over his face—he hates June bugs. Michael pounced on the attack and squashed it with a book. That was not enough for Michael, he was going to protect his little sister as any good big brother would. And so, he became an exterminator, scouring the room for any more of them. He lifted up the bedspread covering my bed, cutting off their access route up to my bed. Then, he sprayed around my room, laying a defensive perimeter for any more bugs that had the idea of messing with the handicapped girl in the middle of the night. The whole ordeal was comical because we made it so. We tried to find the humor in the situation, even though it stemmed from my inability to swat away a simple June bug.

There are so many things I cannot do. I can't lift myself up to see something, I can't wipe my nose, I can't swat a June bug from my face. I can't get my hair out of my face. I have to laugh a little bit about it. When the a June bug is crawling toward my face and I can't swat it away, it is incredibly annoying, but what can you do other than offer it up? One time, I was out on a ride in my chair and I got stuck in the mud. So I had to wait there until someone walked by to ask for their help. If I can't laugh at that image, what can I laugh at?

A positive attitude is critical in dealing with suffering. Sometimes we have to throw our arms up in the air and say, "Thy will be done." If I could shrug, I would. I *can* roll my eyes though; I am very good at that—just ask Paul. Despite the bickering natural to siblings, he taught me how to laugh at myself. He is almost never in a bad mood—there is a happiness in him that is infectious. This happy outlook on everything makes it easier to accept and lift our cross. If we are focused on how terrible everything is at all times, when we are presented with another cross, it will weigh a lot more than if we are moving through life with joy.

CHAPTER 12

Lifting It Up

"Don't waste your suffering."

—Pope St. John Paul II

We hear the phrase "offer it up" a great deal within the context of suffering. I know I heard it from my mom enough times when I'd complain. It can become a battle cry for us when things start getting tough, but I have found that it is often something people say and rarely do. How many times have we said we were going to pray for someone and we never took the time to specifically name them in prayer afterwards? Offering it up is similar in that it is a common prescription, but it is seldom taken. So how do we offer it up; how do we specifically transform suffering into sacrifice? It first requires three things: affliction, intention, and petition.

In the old days, cattle and sheep would be offered up to the gods. Even babies would be sacrificed. This was seen as a tangible gift to the gods of the pagan world that would please them. Christ came and countered that mentality by becoming the gift himself. As such, we call him the Sacrificial Lamb. Tangible sacrifices are still proper, like alms and fasting, but we are able to offer up our suffering as well, which will strengthen our spirit and will. We don't need to kill something for our Lord. Rather, we can take the afflictions that we meet in our life, the pains from our cross, and lift them up. If there is no affliction, there is no sacrifice. Lucky for us, there is no shortage of affliction for any of us. Even the richest man in the world has suffering in his heart that can be dedicated to another and united to our Lord.

Intention is the second component to sacrifice. We must be mindful of others and their struggles rather than being self-absorbed with our own. Just as we would pray for someone, sacrificing for them is a spiritual offering that can help. No one can sacrifice by accident; it has to be a premeditated, intentional act. This takes thought and time to consciously direct ourselves toward that desire. What is important about this component of sacrifice is it takes us out of ourselves. We become vehicles for others. This cannot be done without love, for how will we ever be able to place ourselves at the feet of our Lord for another if not for love?

The intention can be anything, specific or general. Maybe your intention is for someone's general well-being or maybe you tell God to take the suffering for whatever he wants. It can also be applied to a specific issue at hand. It may seem obvious, but it has to be intentional. Although the intention can be general, the desire cannot be vague. The more targeted the intention the more appropriate. Before rushing to make an intention out of the first thing we see, let us spend some time thinking about the person and ask ourselves what they really need. In this way, we are able to pray for things for other people that they would never pray for themselves. Maybe it is a vice that they cannot see because their pride blinds them. Maybe it is for an increase of an already existing virtue in them that they can lean on during a tragedy before them.

My go-to intention is for the priesthood in general or for specific priests in my life. It was the priest that baptized me who told me that my prayers were unique and very beneficial to priests in their vocations. I have taken this very seriously throughout my life. I have had many priests who have been able to recognize the calling to sacrifice for others, and they have always asked or relied on me to pray for them to have the grace to persevere in their vocations. I hope my prayers have contributed to strengthening their resolve to live out their vocations. Other times, though, I don't have a specific intention and specifically request God to decide. This still makes the intention a conscious effort, it is just not of my own choosing. Deciding upon an intention should be a well thought out process, but it is the point where the affliction becomes about another person rather than ourselves.

Lastly, we must fall at the feet of our Lord and bring these pleas to him in prayer. This petition is powerful, for sacrifice preceded it and God the Father is well pleased with those who imitate his Son's love. By following the example of the new Adam and the new Eve, we are able to overcome our own weakened will. Love engenders this sacrificial petition, and through it, we can strengthen not only our relationships with others but with God. We are able to bear our sorrows for others, which transforms those sorrows into joys.

By bringing a petition to our Lord for another, we are able to take the evil of suffering and cleanse it with love. When we turn our suffering into a petition, we triumph over evil. Evil is the source of all suffering whether it be a spiritual evil or a physical evil. Padre Pio tells us that "the most beautiful creed is the one we pronounce in our hour of darkness." When the shadow of suffering descends upon us, we bring light to the struggle when we bring an intentional petition to our Lord.

We must learn how to suffer well. We do this by turning suffering into sacrifice. We must bear an affliction, target an intention, and pray a heartfelt petition. By doing this consciously, we are able to grow in strength and better cope with the sufferings we are dealt. St. Thérèse of Lisieux says, "My whole strength lies in prayer and sacrifice, these are my invincible arms; they can move hearts far better than words."

CHAPTER 13

The Three Seeds

"A beginner must look on himself as one setting out to make a garden for his Lord's pleasure, on most unfruitful soil which abounds in weeds. His Majesty roots up the weeds and will put in good plants instead."

—St. Teresa of Avila

Over the course of my life, there were battles which hindered my normal development. Quite literally, everything takes me longer to do. Patience is something that I have come to need more than anything, not just patience with others but patience with myself. My studies took longer than most people, and it may have been equal parts perfectionism, laziness, and difficulty of the task at hand. I liked all my subjects, for the most part, but I really gravitated towards theology. I chose to major in it because I want to be a saint. Achieving sainthood requires that we grow in holiness. This is a lifelong process that requires us to pray to keep our relationship with God and then to share that relationship with others. We cannot keep it to ourselves; we have to pass it on to those we meet, and that is why theology enriched my life as it did.

I didn't fully understand what a college degree was going to do for me or how it was going to improve my ability to embark on a career in my situation, but I did know that earning a college degree would help me to mature in so many ways. It brought new challenges to my life, and those challenges made me stronger. I was able to find an independence in pursuing a college degree. Each course taught me a little bit about myself and brought new challenges. The courses helped me to mature spiritually in both my relationship with God and the relationships within my family. God gave me new insights into how to relate to family and friends through the courses and the professor's methods for teaching. Taking courses at Ave Maria did allow me a lot of independence because the education allowed me to take my mind to a safe haven, especially if I was facing challenges in the home. It gave me an opportunity to be able to focus on the mental challenges of the education, and in this way, I found freedom from my physical dependency.

I wanted to study so that I didn't feel like I was throwing away an opportunity. Every one of my siblings was able to earn their college degree (except for Paul, who is special), so I was determined that I was not going to be any different. Being at the end of a very large family where I have siblings achieving such great things and their kids doing the same, I wanted to earn my own college degree to show everyone, including myself, that I could do it. One can call it the competitive nature of siblings, and I have enough of them to stay motivated! It was important to me though that I be able to show myself and my family that I could achieve this goal.

It took me eleven years to finish my degree, and attending classes was always a challenge. Through this journey, I was not only able to better come to know God and Mary through my studies, but I was also able to better know myself. I accomplished something that many would say was impossible. This filled me with a tremendous confidence that I could do anything I put my mind to. It was never my mind that was the problem after all.

During this time, alongside my studies, I was also instructed to do something completely out of my comfort zone. We, as a family, spent a lot of time at the Shrine of Our Lady of Czestochowa. I met a priest there named Father Marian who was the pilgrimage director. We became very close and he was a great spiritual guide to me. At times, Father Marian could be very spontaneous and, like any good priest, had a gift for persuading people to do things that they ordinarily did not want to do. One day, he was convinced that I had a gift for public speaking, which was utterly unknown to me. On this occasion, he decided that I should lead a mystery of the Rosary during the daily recitation after Mass. Knowing that I did not have the air volume, I objected to his request and refused to do it on the basis of not being able to project my voice. However, he did not think this was a legitimate excuse, so he held a microphone up to my mouth while I labored to recite a decade of the Rosary. There were not a lot of people present to volunteer and this gave Father Marian an opportunity to convince me to lead a decade. With my unfamiliarity of speaking before crowds and my breathing impairment, his request seemed like an insurmountable challenge, but also a point of anxiety. I prefer to remain inconspicuous as much as possible. However, Fr. Marian did not let me hide the light of Christ, given to me with my faith, under a bushel basket. At every opportunity he got, he made a point of drawing out the goodness in me and constantly encouraged me to witness Christ's love in my life through my words and actions.

One day, Father Marian said to me in his thick Polish accent, "Thérèse, you should write your story. Think of Saint Thérèse, who never left her convent but gave the world a beautiful gift by writing her memoir." I looked at him and laughed. Then I responded, "I don't have anything to say that would be worthwhile to share." He insisted that I write this book, but I was not convinced that God was speaking through him. I thought that he was just flattering me because he loved me so much. In showing his love, he tended to "canonize me," and I thought this took the form of favoritism as opposed to objective guidance in my spiritual life. In hindsight, I think Father Marian was telling me to write my story in order for me to grow spiritually. Yet, at that time, I was not mature enough to see it this way. I was still hiding in the shadow of my parents and using them as an excuse for not emerging into my own life. After much persistence from Father Marian to start this book, I begrudgingly started to write.

Throughout college, I didn't fully understand how many professors and staff members truly cared about my accomplishments because I was not able to be a part of the campus life or attend classes on a regular basis. Attending classes virtually was great in the sense that I could be somewhat part of a given class, but it also gave me a feeling of separation. Many times, I didn't feel part of the school and I didn't know the classmates well. However, after eleven challenging years, I was able to graduate.

Graduation was an incredible moment in my life. Not only the sense of accomplishment but I also had a feeling of overwhelming joy, nostalgia, and bliss. I was able to see in a small way how beneficial it was to put in the time to establish friendships with people at the school. The kindness of the members of the administration was overwhelming to me because they did a great job of providing for my physical needs at graduation. Since I could not sit up for more than two hours, I would have to lay down and rest somewhere during the speeches. They accommodated my needs in an amazing way and reserved a whole section for my family members and friends in addition to providing me with a place to lie down. They provided me with an iPad so I could watch the graduation and know when it was time to receive my diploma. In the beginning, the president made a point of mentioning me during his speech and my academic accomplishments as a quadriplegic. That was stunning to me! While I was overjoyed to get to the moment of receiving my college diploma, I was apprehensive about having to get up on a stage. I had never been in front of so many people at once. Of course, there is a natural insecurity of what they would think of me. I am different and I look different too. It's hard to be put on display when I was, and still am, afraid of such attention. But after the president had mentioned me, the crowd gave me a standing ovation. This was an incredible experience for me, not for the applause, but what would happen next.

In this moment, something incredible happened to me. I heard a voice. Not just anyone's, but it was undoubtedly Mother Teresa's. She said, "I have always been with you. I am here with you now and I will continue to be with you." This was the same woman who visited me in person when I was in a coma in the hospital as a child. She had left me with a miraculous medal that I sleep with every night to this day. She was with me in the middle of the night when I was in a coma, and she was with me during this glorious moment as well. Hearing Mother Teresa's voice was a real consolation and a moment of peace for me as I was able to block out all the applause and focus on her. I had never heard her voice before, and I have a certain amount of skepticism toward such claims. This was clear as day in a moment that I needed it more than ever. And the fact that I was able to know her voice with such certainty provided me with more confidence in the occurrence. This was a beautiful moment in my life, and it far outweighed the glamor of my graduation.

My education taught me a lot about myself, but specifically it watered three seeds in me, which began to grow. The first seed was that I knew that I could be more independent. I was under the care of my parents every moment of every day, and although I needed others' help, I could accomplish something outside of the home. The second seed that began to sprout was a better understanding of God and his calling for me. God is very much still a mystery to me, as he is for all of us, but there was a closeness to him in my studies that granted me better insight into his glorious essence. The third seed was that I found a great deal of fulfillment in the relationships that I developed with the professors, students, and staff members. These were relationships that turned into lasting friendships. These three seeds grew deep within me, and I knew I would have to do the hardest thing I would ever do, something that would bring great suffering to me and my family. But it was something I had to do for God and for myself, for I was beginning to hear his call. I would have to leave home.

CHAPTER 14

The Exodus

*"If any man would come after me, let him deny himself
and take up his cross daily and follow me."*

—Luke 9:23

Every loving family has its challenges. A family unit can
be a source of great suffering in someone's life. Sometimes things happen that can drive a wedge or even sever
the communication lines. Sometimes parents or siblings are
just wrong, and just because we are their child or little sister
doesn't mean we are wrong and they know better than us.
By living the life of a handicapped woman, I am cared for
every minute of the day. This burden was great on my family; everyone in my family had to take care of me at times.

The problem with being a handicapped woman is that
everyone is faced with the question "what is best for Therese?"
on a pretty regular basis. When you aren't physically independent, it is only natural for people (brothers, sisters, and
parents) to forget that I'm mentally and spiritually independent. I am my own person after all. Sometimes in the past,

the family would debate what's best for me, while forgetting to ask me what I wanted. This became a major stress point in my life, for I have a life to live and a unique call from Jesus to answer.

When we love people, we open ourselves up to them. There is a vulnerability there, and they, in a sense, have power over us. When someone we don't know calls us a name, it doesn't really matter. We just feel sorry for them. But when someone we love calls us a name, it hurts deeply because we hold them deeply in our hearts. People can forget the effect they have on those they love.

Over the course of time, I began feeling called to leave the care of my parents. This wasn't like a child going away to college. This was a much bigger deal than that. An endless stream of questions rushed in immediately. Where would I go? Who would care for me? Would I die? What would this do to my parents? All of those questions remained just as the calling did. My parents were getting older and I wanted to achieve a new level of independence. I felt like this was the cross God wanted me to carry, so I had to accept it. I listened to him very closely and spent my due diligence making sure this calling was correct.

I felt somewhat like a witness or a superfluous party to my parent's marriage. I do not say that I should have been more than that to them, or they to me, but rather that I had long since crossed the threshold of childhood and dwelt as an adult within their household. And yet I could not gain the status of a peer. Anyone who has lived in a similar situation can understand this feeling. My parents did not fill the void that I was experiencing on an emotional level—a need for friends to whom I could relate, and with whom I could share, as an equal. I constantly looked to Meg, Kathy, and Charlotte for that kind of support. They were the ones that were available the most to me. It was for this reason that I yearned most for independence. God created us to live in relationship. We, as human beings, depend on others, and they depend upon us. But there is no identity without difference. We are each a unique person with our own individual gifts to share.

Some of my brothers and sisters came to my aid; one in particular offered to take care of me. My oldest sister, Kathy, is a nurse, so it seemed to work out well. When you have such a big family (fifteen children) and there is a hot topic like should Therese leave home, people will take sides, and so unfortunately two sides emerged. Again, throughout my life, many people inside and outside of the family have thought they knew what was best for me. They would forget to ask me though.

My parents were adamantly against me leaving. This wasn't too much of a surprise to me. Looking back on it, my mother, especially, found her identity in taking care of me. If someone gave every waking minute of their day to their children, especially two handicapped ones, moving away from them would deeply affect them too. This would be an unimaginable empty nest for her. My mother was my primary caregiver for forty years. Her strength is saintly. She has performed CPR on me more times than we'd all like to count. She has saved my life countless times and loved me every step of the way. My father has been a rock, as any great father is. He would make modifications to my porta-lung so

I could breathe better, and he would make sure the settings on it were calibrated to how I felt. With so much care and love invested in keeping me alive, it would be impossible for them to let me go.

Paul had left to live with two of my sisters, and they were still coming to grips with that and handling it internally. Caregivers internalize the person they care for and it becomes their purpose. This is because of one thing—love. Remember, when we love someone, we open ourselves to be hurt. We become vulnerable. My parents were definitely hurt by this, and I hate so much that my decision led to their suffering. I felt, and still feel, like it was a calling though. How do I tell my Shepherd that I won't follow him?

I felt like the Israelites at a crossroad. I didn't know what the future would bring, but God did not want me to look back and keep saying "What if." I may have been wandering out into the desert for a long time before I found my destination. Yet I felt the calling and so I had to follow. I found perspective in the Gospels when Peter walked on water. He had to keep his eyes fixed on Jesus if he wanted to make it across the lake safely. This is what my brother, Father Peter, and my sister, Kathy, kept telling me, "Keep your eyes fixed on Jesus, Therese. Don't look back. It is your decision to make. You have to choose to get out of the boat and walk on water with your eyes centered on Jesus." This was a tough decision to make. There was nothing "comfortable" about it, but I think the lesson Jesus wanted me to learn is that loving your cross does not mean we will find comfort and pleasure in this world, only in the next. I had to learn this lesson for myself in order to be able to preach the message of faith and trust in God with authenticity.

So I was trapped. It's not like I could walk out the front door and run away from home. I would have to be physically taken somewhere else, and if my parents weren't going to let me go, then what could I do? A small group of brothers and sisters came to my aid. One day, when my parents were at adoration, they came into the house, packed up my clothes, and loaded me into the van. Within a short period of time, they got me on an airplane. Yes, my brothers and sisters, literally, smuggled me from my own parent's house. This exodus was the hardest thing I ever experienced. I have never experienced such emotional suffering before in my life. I had to accept my cross though, the one that God had called me to carry—not the one anyone in my family thought I should carry. There have been years of struggles in my family over this exodus, and it is very much an open wound, but as with any loving family, we try to mend the wound.

Family breeds friction. Every family has it. There is too much love in that unit to not have suffering. We take everything personally because it is personal. The roots of that love run so deep. One place a family can always go for comfort and harmony is prayer. A family doesn't argue over the words of the Rosary. They may argue over what to have for breakfast or which movie to watch, but they can't dispute something like prayer. I know that my parents and brothers and sisters are praying for me, as I continue to pray for them every day. There is still pain, but that comes from this cross that I have accepted. In many ways, this cross is heavier than the cross of spinal meningitis. But I must lift it and love it, for this cross, like all crosses, was an invitation to grow closer with God. How could anyone say no to that?

CHAPTER 15

Saintly Examples

"If you really want to love Jesus, first learn to suffer,
because suffering teaches you to love."

—St. Gemma Galgani

Sometimes, the crosses we bear defy logic, but that is suffering, isn't it? If it made sense, it wouldn't hurt so badly. The age-old question comes to mind yet again: why does God allow good people to suffer? We can look to the saints, many of which had to deal with intense suffering.

The first saint that comes to mind is my patron saint, the Little Flower, Saint Thérèse of Lisieux. As one who suffered with the physical ailments of tuberculosis as well as the emotional pain of losing her mother, St. Thérèse is an example of a suffering servant who trusted God to carry her crosses with her. She beautifully points out how suffering is the way to life in God when she says, "Jesus offers you the cross, a very heavy cross, and you are afraid of not being able to carry it without giving way. Why? Our Beloved Himself fell three times on the way to Calvary, and why should we not imitate Him?"[3]

The Little Flower tells us that if we trust in Jesus, we have nothing to fear about suffering. In his passion, death, and resurrection, Jesus conquered sin and death. Jesus loved us so much that he sacrificed his own life for our salvation. St. Thérèse exemplified a dedicated spouse in that she gave her total self as a bride to Christ. I feel spiritually drawn to her as my patron saint because she suffered in many of the ways that I have suffered. She points out that Christ did the hard work of redeeming man from sin and if we share in his sufferings, he will help us through the most impossible situations. In her writings, St. Thérèse points out the uselessness in thinking that we can get to heaven without suffering when she says, "Do not imagine that love can be found without suffering, for we carry with us our human nature; and yet, what a source of merit it is!"[4] This interpretation tends to focus on how we feel about suffering instead of taking into account the redemptive merits of suffering. If we unite our sufferings with Christ and have him ever in our sight during these trials, we come to a deeper understanding of the cross. This deeper understanding of the cross leads us to imitate the love that Christ showed for us in choosing death and new life through his cross and resurrection.

3   Father Bob Colaresi, *Daily Reflections by Saint Therese of Lisieux* (Society of the Little Flower, 2017), accessed March 5, 2017, http://www.littleflower.org/prayers-sharing/daily-reflections/?dateOfReflection=1/29/2017.

4   Ibid.

Saint Bernadette may have discovered the healing waters of Lourdes, but she is another saint who faced a great deal of suffering in her life. She is in fact the patron saint of the sick. As an adult, she suffered from a tubercular tumor in the bone of her knee. People came and asked her why she did not seek healing from the very miraculous waters she found that had healed so many. She responded that it was her business to be ill. St. Bernadette was given a great miracle, from which came miracles, yet she never tested those waters for herself. She had discovered the cure and had shared it with the world but never tried it for herself. She embraced her suffering and truly loved the cross she bore because she knew it drew her closer to God. She provides an incredible perspective on suffering when she says, "Why must we suffer? Because here below pure Love cannot exist without suffering. O Jesus, Jesus, I no longer feel my cross when I think of yours."

St. Bernadette had a great deal of suffering, for as a child she contracted cholera and had severe asthma. She also experienced the emotional suffering of being rejected by others when she brought her apparitions to light. St. Bernadette is a great example of a saint who dedicated her suffering to the Lord.

Another great saint that we can look to as an example of how to suffer is St. Gemma Galgani. She is not as popular of a saint, but she suffered a great deal from many things. I find her to be a special saint because she suffered with spinal meningitis as I have. In her writings, she talks about when the doctors discovered the curvature in her spine. I remember when I was ten or eleven years old and the doctors told my mom and me that my curvature would become increasingly worse in my teen years. When I turned thirteen, their predictions did indeed come true. This was evident in a pulmonary evaluation where the pulmonologist told me I was going to die very soon because my breathing capacity was impaired. As one can imagine, this was terrifying for a thirteen-year-old, but I found comfort in St. Gemma as she suffered so much as a young girl. Her spinal meningitis was healed as well, which she would attribute to the Sacred Heart of Jesus. St. Gemma's suffering was only beginning though. When she was eighteen, she became an orphan and took on the responsibility of raising seven younger siblings. At age twenty-one, she was given the stigmata, an unbelievable agony I cannot fathom. She explains the vision that occurred when she received her stigmata.

> She opened her mantle and covered me with it. At the same moment Jesus appeared with His wounds open: but instead of blood, flames as it were of fire seemed to issue from them. In an instant those flames touched my hands and feet and heart. I felt as if I were dying and should have fallen to the floor, had not my Mother supported me under her mantle. I remained in that position some hours. Then she kissed my forehead, the vision disappeared and I found myself on my knees alone: but I still felt intense pain in my hands, feet, and heart. I rose to go to bed, but I found that blood was flowing from the places where I had the pain. I covered them as well as I could and got into bed with the help of my Guardian Angel. Next morning I

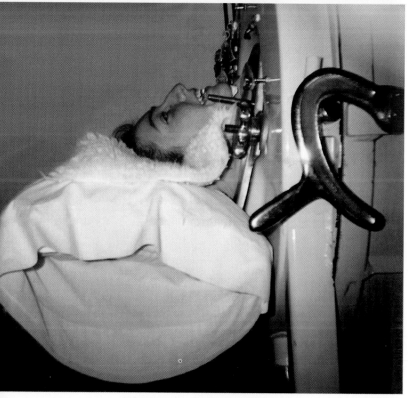

Therese in the iron lung

Patty and Therese

Michael, Patty, Paul, & Therese (1977)

Dad doing aquatic exercises with Therese – Sanibel Island, FL

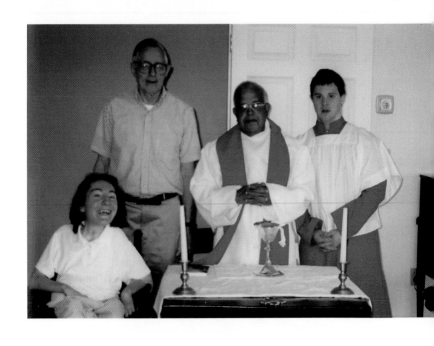

Mom holding Therese in
a pool – Marco Island,
FL 1990s

Joe, Therese, & Paul at Disney World (1980s)

Patty & Therese (1980)

Favorite pastime - Playing Fisher Price

Dad, Paul, & Therese

Liz & Therese

Joe putting necklace on Therese – Pilgrimage to Guadalupe (1987)

Left to right: Cedric Meeschaert, Michael, Amity (cousin), Dad, Mom, Therese, Laurent Meeschaert, & Joe
Mexico (1987)

Paul's & Therese's confirmation

Patty & Therese – Greenwich, CT (1980)

Williams Family
Back left to right: Charlotte, Diane, Peter, Mary, Meg, Patty, Laurie, &
David
Center left to right: Daddy Bob, Grambese, Loretta & Spencer, Mom &
Dad
Front left to right: Michael, Joe, Paul, Liz, Chris, & Therese

Therese at May Crowning in Newton Centre, MA (1983-84)

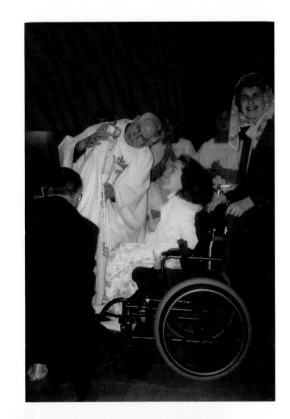

May Crowning with
Fr. Marian – Shrine of
Our Lady Czestochowa
Doylestown, PA (1997)

Fr. Rafal (friend), Therese, & Paul at Meg's home in New Hampshire
(1998-99)

Playing cards (1999-2000)

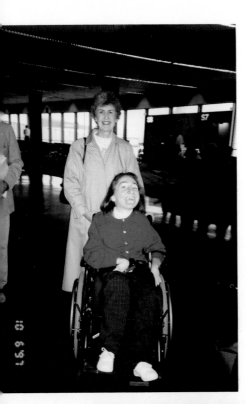

Mom & Therese travel-
ing (early 2000s)

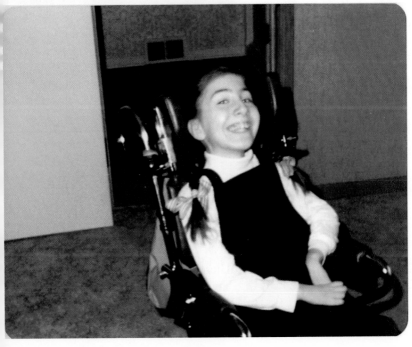

Dr. Maria Fedoryka (Therese's philosophy professor)

found it difficult to go to Holy Communion. I put on
a pair of gloves to hide my hands. But I could scarcely
stand, and felt every moment that I should die.[5]

Why would God give such people his wounds? Why
would he offer this cross to bear? This is the mystery of suffering manifested through an incredible miracle. St. Gemma,
through the stigmata, was literally united to Christ's suffering
on the cross. Shortly after receiving the stigmata, she contracted tuberculosis at age twenty-five and passed away. St.
Gemma lived with continual suffering in her life. Although
her life was short, she never lost her faith and found love in
her suffering and dedicated her pain to God.

I have always had a great devotion to Mother Teresa—a
special bond of sorts. As previously mentioned, she came to
visit me in the middle of the night at the hospital while I
was in a coma. What drew her to that hospital at that hour?
There was no evidence of her being there other than a phone
call to my parents and a miraculous medal left behind. I
sleep to this day with that miraculous medal taped to my
porta-lung above my head. Mother Teresa is a special saint
to me because not only did she bear her cross but she also
comforted the suffering in such a proximate and selfless way.
Mother Teresa and her nuns suffer with those who suffer.
They do not live a life of lavishness—they live in the dirt
with the poorest of the poor. Mother Teresa told us that
"pain and suffering have come into your life, but remember

5   Joan Carroll Cruz, *Mysteries, Marvels, Miracles in the Lives of Saints*
     (Charlotte: TAN Books, 1997).

pain, sorrow, suffering are but the kiss of Jesus—a sign that you have come so close to Him that He can kiss you."

It has been discovered from her letters that she had spent a major portion of her life bearing a dark night of the soul. This is the most unimaginable kind of suffering. A soul that is so pious and holy, constantly bidding her Father's will, could not see him. A story goes that she was in adoration with her spiritual advisor and she passed a note to him during their holy hour. The note read, "Where is Jesus, I cannot see His face?" This was in front of the Blessed Sacrament. How could such a saint not recognize the face of Jesus in the Eucharist if it weren't for such a dark night of the soul? After the holy hour, her spiritual advisor confronted her about the note and asked how she couldn't see Jesus's face in the Eucharist. She asked him if he wanted to see how she sees the face of Jesus. After responding that he did, she led him out onto a street in Calcutta. She began bathing a leper. After cleaning the man's open sores, she looked up from him and said, "This is how I see the face of Jesus."

When we accept our cross, we are able to better see the face of Jesus. Mother Teresa's cross to bear was not only her dark night but caring for the sick and suffering. By accepting that cross with an open heart of faith, she can better see Jesus. Maybe it is why St. Bernadette refused to go to the healing waters of Lourdes. Maybe it is why God gave St. Gemma the stigmata. We will never fully understand the mystery of suffering, but we do know that if we accept it like the saints who accepted theirs, we are better able to see Jesus Christ. We must accept our cross because from it, we will suffer the right things and it will bring us closer to God. In short, one could say that suffering empties us so that Christ can fill us.

Prayer for Accepting Your Cross

Lord, I accept the cross you have given me, and I trust that you will use my suffering in the best way. This cross I am suffering now has a purpose. I trust that you will give it purpose and I offer it up for love of you and for the salvation of those who are in most need of your mercy. I love you and I give my life to you knowing that you will use my suffering to redeem the worst of sinners. I being at the top of the list. I grieve with you at the sins of impurity, hatred, anger, malice, and all the many sins that bring you much sorrow and pain. I ask your Holy Mother Mary to comfort me as she comforted you on the road to Calvary. I ask her to suffer with me and for me to bring me peace and joy that only a mother can give in the midst of suffering and pain. Amen.

PART III

Carry Your Cross

CHAPTER 16

Ongoing Suffering

"If God causes you to suffer much, it is a sign that He has great designs for you, and that He certainly intends to make you a saint."

—St. Ignatius of Loyola

Carrying our cross is an ongoing effort, one that will continue until we reach our death. Although this thought is morbid, it is true, and we need to understand that we are going to meet suffering in different ways for our entire life. I have lived with the same handicap my whole life, but the issues I must contend with have evolved as I have aged. Our bodies change, and as mine changes, it slowly contracts and grows weaker. Any aging person can say the same thing, but as my body's starting point was so disadvantaged, I must face an increasing number of ongoing challenges.

For instance, I have contractures in my neck, back, left hand, and my legs. This is where my muscles and tendons have shortened and tightened. I cannot stretch out my hand, so most of my typing is done with my knuckle. Both my hips have been out of their sockets from the beginning, but as I get older, I find that my right leg has stiffened. This affects my flexibility, especially in my back, which has changed my shape. This is important because my wheelchair is custom molded to my back, so as my scoliosis increases, I can't fit to the chair anymore. I believe that I also have arthritis now and I am feeling the effects of it in my left hand, which is paralyzed. Also, if I contract a respiratory infection, it can be very serious for me, even life-threatening. A simple cold has always been a terrible suffering. It can easily turn into pneumonia, resulting in visits to the emergency room.

Anything related to my reproductive system has always been an ongoing challenge for me. That is not to say that every woman does not suffer with the same hardships, but menopause has been very difficult. Not only do I have the same constant flux of hormones as others, but I have intense and unbearable pain when my ovary and uterus become inflamed. The pain comes from all these organs being together in a tight space, scrunched up against my other abdominal organs. It feels like someone is stabbing me with a knife. This discomfort breeds constant nausea and headaches.

Apart from the status of my body, daily functions remain an ongoing struggle. Going to the bathroom has been a life-long struggle which only becomes harder with age. I need someone to physically press on my stomach to help. This requires a great deal of strength and certainly isn't pleasant. As previously mentioned, I need to be suctioned up to twelve times a day. This will always be one of the most painful routines I face on a daily basis.

I believe that God loves me enough to allow me to suffer and to experience in a very small way how he suffered at the crucifixion. That may sound presumptuous, but I believe that he chooses certain people in this life to suffer and to sacrifice in the way that he sacrificed because he loves us. We have seen this in some of the saints, whom he gifted the stigmata. In no way am I comparing my handicap to the stigmata, but it does show us that God chooses some to suffer in a special way. This suffering is my vocation. I am called to carry this cross, and I will gladly take on any more he wants to offer, but I will only accept the crosses Jesus chooses to give me, not the ones I give myself or others give me. I know full well that Jesus will be with me to carry any cross that he gives me. Jesus is my greatest teacher in how to suffer. If I want to know how to suffer well, I don't need to look anywhere else but to a crucifix. I can say, "He was whipped. He was spat on. He was kicked. He was betrayed. He was ridiculed, insulted, blasphemed against. What am I griping about?"

Beyond the physical, my handicap creates situations that have very sensitive context. Many people are invested in me in a very special way, from my family to my friends to my caregivers. I believe that they find their vocation in taking care of me. So knowing that not only do I have to carry my cross but that I am someone else's cross to bear is a very difficult thing to understand.

I spend most of my days lying on a table in the family room. When I was a child, I would lay on the kitchen table since that was the major intersection of our house. I was able to observe my family in a very special and intimate way. My world was my vicinity. In many ways, it still is, but humans are supposed to be mobile and able to achieve independence. The denial of these two basic privileges is a constant reality that I face. These ongoing struggles are the daily crosses to bear. Some are heavier than others. Some are more frequent than others, but it is by them that I come to the Father.

CHAPTER 17

Ongoing Temptations

"Do not grieve over the temptations you suffer. When the Lord intends to bestow a particular virtue on us, He often permits us first to be tempted by the opposite vice. Therefore, look upon every temptation as an invitation to grow in a particular virtue and a promise by God that you will be successful, if only you stand fast."

—St. Philip Neri

The devil targets the vulnerable. Not only do I hear his nagging temptations in my head, but he also may have interfered in the physical world in his attacks on me. Whenever there has been a problem with my ventilators, Mom would always say, "The devil is attacking." That could be very true! I would not deny that he tries to attack me when I am the most vulnerable.

However, I don't believe in giving him that much credit and allowing him the power to control that kind of situation. I try to turn these moments of a negative and awful situation into a moment of real concentrated prayer where I ask God to take control and fix the ventilator. God can do anything.

91

He is in control of both material and spiritual things. God allows the devil to have some ability to interfere in our lives so that we can have an opportunity to put our faith in God. I believe that if the devil has the power to destroy material things, then God certainly has the power to stop him. We must invite God to do so.

When we suffer, a feeling of abandonment lays root, and this creates opportunities for more fear and doubts to completely overcome our spirit. We tend to blame God in these moments. I think God is an easy target when it comes to laying blame. We feel that he is invisible. We can't see his physical presence amongst us, so the instinct is, "Why not blame an invisible entity?" After all, he can't feel the pain of blame and he becomes the scapegoat to suppress our rising emotions.

The devil likes to use these negative feelings we have toward our spiritual demise. I am acutely aware of the devil's delight in using my suffering against me. During such times, I try to look into my interior life and ask myself the question, "Am I going to let the devil rule me? Or am I going to turn to Jesus, the source of mercy, healing, and compassion?" If I am honest with myself, I can look at a crucifix and say with all certainty, "He knows every human suffering, and I am not alone in my pain. He has given me numerous loving people in my life to help me deal with this pain." I really do not like to consciously succumb to self-pity, but this is a feeling I am constantly fighting against in my spiritual life.

The devil uses suffering as an opportunity to spring on the attack. This is an appeal to our pride, much like the first temptation of Eve in the garden. We must keep our defenses up, for that time of suffering is an opportunity for sacrificial love. Satan wants to distract us from that by filling our heads with questions like, "Why is God doing this to me?" and "How could he turn his back on me like this?" We must prepare ourselves for such temptations with prayer and devotion, specifically to St. Michael the Archangel. The name Micah, or Michael, means "Who is like God?" It is said that this was his reply to Lucifer when Satan was tempting other angels to rebel against God. He is specifically named in the Book of Revelation as the leader of the angels fighting Satan and the other demons, casting them out of heaven: "Now war arose in heaven, Michael and his angels fighting against the dragon; and the dragon and his angels fought, but they were defeated and there was no longer any place for them in heaven. And the great dragon was thrown down, that ancient serpent, who is called the Devil and Satan, the deceiver of the whole world—he was thrown down to the earth, and his angels were thrown down with him" (Rv 12:7–9).

It was Pope Leo XIII who had a vision of St. Michael and wrote the prayer to him that we would come to know so well. He asked that it be recited after every Low Mass (in the Tridentine or Latin form) in 1886. This prayer is the most common plea for St. Michael's help in the war between good and evil. St. Michael is usually depicted with a sword in his hand standing on the serpent's head. The devil seeks our spiritual destruction in the daily events of our lives. The primary means by which he seeks our destruction is spiritual, since God has given us spiritual immortality and promised the resurrection of our bodies. So the devil tries to separate us from God by tempting us to disobedience through lies.

Hence, he is also known as the "Father of Lies." The first lie, as recorded in the Book of Genesis, is the seed of suspicion—that God is not good, and that he is not doing what is best for us. "But God said, 'You shall not eat of the fruit of the tree which is in the midst of the garden, neither shall you touch it, lest you die.' But the serpent said to the woman, 'You will not die. For God knows that when you eat of it your eyes will be opened, and you will be like God, knowing good and evil'" (Gn 3:3–5).

In an attempt to lead us astray, the devil plants seeds of doubt and despair in our minds and hearts by telling us we are not truly loved by God. But we have an advocate in St. Michael. Whenever I feel like I am being attacked by the devil, I call on St. Michael to wage war against Satan and all the evil spirits who prowl about the world seeking the ruin of souls. My devotion to St. Michael is a firmly planted cornerstone of my spirituality.

We don't think in terms of living and fighting a spiritual battle on a daily basis. The mindset of our culture is to deny the devil's existence while at the same time believing that we human beings don't have any control over our dispositions. The tendency is to just throw up our hands and say to ourselves, "This is a horrible situation. There's nothing I can do about it. I give up. Life is horrible. There is no God. God doesn't love me." All of these thoughts give power to the devil. We have been fed the lie that the devil doesn't exist. To deny Satan's existence is to give him power. He can then attack us under the cover of our own ignorance. I would even go further and say that denying his existence becomes an invitation to him.

I think the most important way of handling any kind of suffering is to acknowledge immediately that God is alive and well, and that we can control our thoughts and invite God to take control of a bad situation. We can choose to use our God-given gift of reason to step back and pray for the grace to shine a positive light on the situation at hand. This is a conscious act of the will. Rather than dropping our head, we lift it to heaven where we place our trust. This allows God to bring peace to turmoil. Remember that Christ "rebuked the wind, and said to the sea, 'Peace! Be still!' And the wind ceased, and there was a great calm" (Mk 4:39). He can do the same to our hearts when a storm brews overhead. In this peace, we are more likely to find a solution to the problem.

Many people run from bad situations, but I literally cannot. Believe it or not, this has been somewhat of a blessing since it forces me to face the situation head on. From there, I can invite God into the situation to ease my burden. If I allow the devil to have free reign over my thoughts, then I am not going to be open to prayer with God. We must monitor our thoughts with discipline. We are responsible for them and they can lead us down a dark path. We must maintain zeal and stay far away from apathy, for it is in this complacency that the devil tempts me to give up my cross. He tells me that it's too heavy. That I don't need to carry that load. That God gave it to me and so God doesn't love me. He will try every trick in the book, and if we don't condition our thoughts to be steadfast and strong in faith, then he will find a way in.

The reality is each of us fights a spiritual battle every minute of every day. This fight is for our soul. We are faced with moral choices each day. Are we on God's side or the devil's? Are we somewhere in between? Someone who chooses the devil throws down their crosses and may refuse to live another day with suffering. We can unfortunately see this as the suicide rate continues to rise. The devil has been able to stray so many people away from God because they do not value suffering. There is so much value to suffering in terms of our faith. There are many kinds of chronic illnesses that people live with every day and they don't even understand the spiritual value of that suffering. They just try to numb the pain with medication. I understand the merits of suffering but I only understand it because I have chosen to train my mind to go toward the spiritual, to go toward God in my suffering. If we don't engage in spiritual exercises like this, then we will not be strong in our faith.

Exercising does not feel good right away, but once we've formed a habit of doing it, then it begins to feel good. We actually gain some vitality back. The same applies to doing spiritual exercises. It may not feel good to pray, to fast a little bit, to go to confession on a regular basis, or to go to Mass frequently. We may be lethargic about it at first, but if we work it into our daily routines, we will then begin to feel alive in the Spirit. This is so important for loving the cross. To love the cross, we need the Holy Spirit to play an active part in our lives. We need the Holy Spirit to be able to embrace suffering and to see suffering as a means of intimately uniting ourselves with Jesus.

CHAPTER 18

Pushing Forward to Calvary

"The road is narrow. He who wishes to travel it more easily
must cast off all things and use the cross as his cane."

—St. John of the Cross

Once we find our cross and lift it, the last thing we must do is carry our cross toward our Calvary. The Way of the Cross is a beautiful allegory for our lives, and we must carry our cross till our death. But there are times that we let go of our cross and times we aren't the most faithful disciple to our Lord. Maybe we neglect a responsibility of parenthood or marriage. Every sin drives a wedge between us and our vocation. So every sin is not just a sin against God, it is a sin against those that you are bound to in your vocation. What is most important in this time is to run to confession, receive our Lord's forgiveness, and pick the cross up again.

No one can suffer their whole life. For their own survival, they must offer it up in love for another. Someone can sacrifice for their whole lives and they will live a very happy life that is drawn closer to God each and every day. But if someone sits in their own misery and wallows in their own suffering, they will not find any hope in what is to come. They will despair and they will either end their physical life or their spiritual life. Conversely, if they learn to offer their suffering up, it can be a new beginning of an alleviated physical life or a deepened spiritual life.

If we refuse to carry our cross, it is a sin that affects the world. By refusing to carry it, we are telling God that we do not trust him and that we really do not care to be with him for all eternity. We can see examples of this in our world today. The sin of abortion is the refusal to accept all the hardships and suffering that go into conceiving, giving birth, and raising children. Abortion affects the whole community. We can also see the effects of sin in the disgusting behavior of many of our bishops and priests. Their behavior is a refusal to accept the cross of their vocations as priests. Whether they chose to become priests because they thought it was going to bring them an easy life of comfort and pleasure or whether they dropped their crosses somewhere along the way in their vocations, it comes to the same point. It is a refusal to carry the cross of the priesthood. One man's public sin affects the whole community. So we must carry ourselves not only for our own fulfillment and happiness but for the common good of all.

We know that offering up suffering takes affliction, intention, and petition, but sometimes the hardest thing is putting one foot in front of the other. We can often doubt ourselves and feel like giving up. We grow fatigued and are beaten down in our suffering. Our endurance is tested and a great amount of perseverance is needed in this effort. The road to Calvary is never easy. God traveled it himself, and even he fell three times along it. But he always got back up, accepted his cross again, and marched forward with sacrificial love in every step.

There are four primary sources of spiritual perseverance to draw from for that perilous journey. We first need to establish a deep and consistent prayer life—only then will we be able to bring our suffering to God and our sacrifices to others. We need to form virtues, for the road to Calvary calls upon each and every one at different times. We need others on which to lean. Our family and friends are there for us and will serve as our Simon of Cyrene as we carry our cross. Lastly, we need the Eucharist. By attending Mass and holy adoration, we are better able to unite ourselves to Jesus Christ. He becomes our support and feeds us the spiritual strength needed to continue on as he did. When we have these four things, we are able to walk as Christ did.

CHAPTER 19

Prayerful Dialogue

*"For me prayer is a surge of the heart, it is a simple
look towards Heaven, it is a cry of recognition and
of love, embracing both trial and joy."*

—St. Thérèse of Lisieux

The power of prayer is something that we continue to discover as our suffering deepens. In a world that is all about the external, it is more critical than ever to withdraw ourselves and retreat to an internal dialogue with God. My handicap makes people less accessible. I can't go meet them for coffee. I couldn't have a sleepover when I was kid. Technology has helped with this, but communication is still a slow and arduous task. But I don't need a keyboard to talk to God. I don't need to meet him for coffee or arrange a sleepover to deepen our relationship. I just need to clear my mind and approach him internally with my requests and thanks.

Prayer is conversation with God, so when we pray, we learn how to trust in him for the answers to problems in our lives. In my prayer life, I ask Jesus and Mary to tell me what they want me to do or say, and I listen for their response. Our prayer life should be a dialogue, not just a monologue! We should be conversing with God in prayer just as we converse with our parents, our brothers and sisters, and our close friends. We make a lot of time for talking with human beings, but do we take the same amount of time to talk with God? How can we learn to trust in God if we don't take the time to converse with him and get to know who we are supposed to be trusting? God is Truth. God doesn't ever lie to us, so we can always trust him to know what is best for us. God never hurts us and he never betrays us. Maybe it feels like he is far away at times, but these are the times he gives us the freedom to choose to follow his guidance.

Habit is such an important thing to form in preparation for the inevitable suffering that lies before us. Forming the correct spiritual habits now is critical so that we are well equipped for the later stretches of our road to Calvary. Prayer needs to become habit—an intentional, consistent dedication of time and focus for our Lord.

The easiest way to form this habit is a daily Rosary. We have all prayed it, but I can attest to the fact that its power grows once it becomes habit. When I say the Rosary consistently, I find myself reaching a deeper state of prayer. I become content and comforted by our Lady and gain an invaluable perspective on what I am praying for. When I reach that place, there is no suffering.

Another important daily habit to establish is the morning offering. Beginning the day offering up the day to God through the intercession of the Blessed Mother is essential for enduring the cross. After the day is done, it is just as important to perform an examination of conscience. This self-reflection shows us not just what we did wrong, but also what we did right. By bookending our day with prayer, our friendship with Jesus deepens.

Our Lady has always been with me on this journey, like a mother caressing her child. There were some pretty frightening times when I was at death's door and our Lady interceded, restoring me to health. For example, I could not breathe without the assistance of a respirator and I would grind my teeth in fear and panic when I couldn't breathe. My survival instinct tells me to hang on, even when it seems like there is no hope of regaining the ability to breathe. The Blessed Mother has used my mother so many times to restore me to health. Together, they have cared for me in a way most mothers don't have to care for their child.

My parents' prayer life is an incredibly unique thing. I watched them up close and personal praying for over forty years, and it is truly a sight to behold. My dad has a great deal of obsessive compulsiveness, so he cannot help himself when it comes to sticking to his routine. If people with OCD are good at anything, it is forming habits! The habits he formed around his prayer life are amazing. He has a discipline of saying nine Rosaries a day. Yes, nine! Although he didn't force us to say nine growing up, the roots of my prayer life run deep due to his spiritual leadership. Being the staunch individual that he is, he did his best to impress those strict habits on his children. I was very blessed to have him as a father. My parents taught me the language of prayer. If I hadn't become fluent in that language, I would have no idea where I would be today.

The nice thing about the Rosary is that it is a prayer that can be memorized. I do not need to have a booklet in front of me to pray it. Wherever I am, whatever I am doing, I can stop and say a Rosary or even just one decade. When I take rides in my chair alone, I typically pray a Rosary because it is a great time to be alone with the Blessed Mother and the Trinity and to have conversations with them. While sitting in my chair, I cannot physically use rosary beads to keep track of how many Hail Marys I say, so I count them in my head. Sometimes I get so distracted by the beauty of God's creation around me as I am conversing with God and his Mother that I lose my place in the Rosary. My conversations with God have sometimes also turned into conversations with myself, with God as the bystander. Consequently, I always take longer praying a Rosary than I should. It is a good thing that God knows me and does not care if I lose my place because I can always pick up where I left off.

Our prayer should also be open and honest. We should not be scared to express our emotions to God in prayer. We must bring him our worries and frustrations. If we are doubting his plan for us, we must tell him. If we are angry that something didn't go our way, we must tell him. The devil wants us to turn our backs on him. We must stay with him through the good times and the bad times and not hesitate to directly bring him our concerns, even if they be with his plan.

My spiritual director opened my heart to seeking an intimate, one-on-one relationship with Jesus when he pointed out that I should ask God questions concerning both big and little things. It is like asking someone for directions when you don't know where you are going. Most people wouldn't refuse to tell you how to get somewhere, so why would God? In our household, the idea of trust was like the old saying, "God helps those who help themselves." "Jesus, I trust in you" was a nice saying, but not well practiced. Dad often said, "If you need a helping hand, there's one at the end of your arm." The hand at the end of my paralyzed arm is less than ideal.

I ask God to direct my steps and practice the discipline of quieting my mind when it starts to worry. We must not let worry and anxiety lay root, for that is a habit of a weakened will. We must conquer this weakness through submitting our will to God's. Worry must be replaced by trust in God. And God tells us explicitly not to worry when he says, "Therefore I tell you, do not be anxious about your life, what you shall eat or what you shall drink, nor about your body, what you shall put on. Is not life more than food, and the body more than clothing? Look at the birds of the air: they neither sow nor reap nor gather into barns, and yet your heavenly Father feeds them. Are you not of more value than they?" (Mt 6:25–26).

Prayer throws these worries away, but it must be intentional. It must be an act of the will and intellect. We don't pray with our mouths. We pray with our souls. Withdrawing ourselves from this world and reaching out to God from the inside out fosters in us a power needed to carry our cross. Forming this habit is the first, most crucial thing to develop when we look up our road to Calvary. We will never get there without prayer. Our legs will grow wobbly for lack of a strong foundation, and we will waver and fall off the road. A steadfast commitment to a deeper prayer life grants us this strong foundation on which we can grow in virtue to carry our cross for our Lord.

CHAPTER 20

Virtue

*"You must accept your cross; if you bear it
courageously, it will carry you to heaven."*

—St. John Vianney

A personal and well-developed prayer life yields the virtues needed to lighten our cross as we journey toward our Lord. Each is unique and each is necessary. Some come more easily to us, based on our personalities, while others seem impossible, but all things are possible through Christ. He gave the blind sight, he gave light to the darkness, and he died for the sins of the very people who put him to death. Christ has proven time and time again in the Gospels that anything can be obtained through him. We just must not be afraid to ask.

The first virtue to foster is Faith, for it is essential to any man or woman who is carrying their cross. "Now faith is the assurance of things hoped for, the conviction of things not seen" (Heb 11:1). We must understand that God's providential plan for us will make sense in time and will lead us to a better life. We must realize that our plans will be disrupted and we will be asked to carry our cross, but that cross has a very special purpose. There is nothing wrong with planning our day, week, or year so long as we understand that God has his own plan and we must yield to it. My situation does not afford me the ability to plan anything, because I require the assistance of others to carry out the plan. So what other choice do I really have but to trust in God?

Hope is our eyesight towards what is to come. Some people, when carrying their cross, look up the road and only see Calvary. They don't see the sun peeking out on the horizon beyond it or the light of the Kingdom shining upon them. If we can't feel the warmth from the light of hope, then we will never understand the love behind God's plan for us. Jesus Christ gave his life for our salvation and is calling us to be with him in his eternal paradise. I am a living witness of this hope. I have seen that light, felt that warmth, and heard that call. I am hopeful for my future, and I hope that it is one that will extend into an eternal communion with my Father.

We all desire to love and be loved as we were made in our Creator's image and likeness. John tells us in his first letter, "Beloved, let us love one another; for love is of God, and he who loves is born of God and knows God. He who does not love does not know God; for God is love" (1 Jn 4:7–8). There is no love without self-giving. There are so many people today who yearn for love but are so guarded that they cannot give themselves. They are guarded because they are scared of being hurt—they are terrified of suffering. Maybe it was how they were raised or societal influences, but they want all of the benefits of love without the sacrifices of it.

Let's consider our Lord in this context. As he is God, his divine nature could have just willed our salvation, but Jesus was also a man. He had to love as a human as well, which means sacrifice was necessary. Jesus had to die on the cross because there is no true act of love without a sacrifice of the self. Through this life, we must unite ourselves to our Lord and offer the pains of our suffering for others. We must not only love our cross as the opportunity it is but love *from* our cross as we endure the pain of our sacrifices for others.

One of the virtues that may not come naturally to us is fortitude. According to the *Catechism*, "Fortitude is the moral virtue that ensures firmness in difficulties and constancy in the pursuit of the good" (CCC 1808). We see great examples of fortitude in the martyrs of the Church, who remained firm despite the danger before them. Fortitude is a virtue which only God can give. We cannot manufacture this kind of courage. Rather, we have to ask God for this grace because with fortitude, we are able to persevere in the darkest times. Just as every person is different, so too does every person have their own fears. Believe me, I have my own set of fears, but persevering in prayer helps me find the courage I need to overcome whatever fears are holding me back from doing God's will. We all have fears that we need to overcome, and the secret to overcoming fear is to ask for the grace to be bold witnesses to God's love in the world. It is my experience that God responds to this request with the virtue of fortitude.

In many ways, it is harder to live a saintly life today than it was in the Middle Ages. We can indulge our every pleasure at the click of a button. Through technology and the enormous wealth that we have as a nation, we can very easily satisfy every temporal desire. Temperance becomes so much more important in this digital age. When so much is available to us at every turn, it takes a tremendous amount of self-regulation to remain moderate. If we indulge the body, we will live by the body. My situation is unique in that my body forces me to be moderate in all things. My diet has always been an important part of maintaining my health. In large part, an imbalanced diet can adversely affect my breathing. It is frustrating to me when I hear someone complaining about something that is a mild inconvenience. When someone *suffers* over being denied a luxury (because they have spoiled themselves rotten through years of greedy behavior), how will they ever be able to endure true suffering when they meet it? Over indulgence makes us soft. Temperance strengthens us so that we are armed and ready for when suffering makes its attack.

Humility is also an important ingredient to carrying our cross, for it reminds us that we are not in control. We cannot understand that God is in control if we do not first understand that we are not. Saint Augustine tells us, "It was pride that changed angels into devils; it is humility that makes men as angels." We live with a certain amount of humility, but I don't believe anyone lives in complete resignation to the will of God. We all have pride in our hearts. Maybe we are proud of our accomplishments, and there is nothing wrong with that so long as they remember that nothing is possible without God. It is important for us to keep God in mind not just through our sufferings but also through our victories so that we can maintain a humble life, cognizant of God's will. Pride brought about the first sin and thus the suffering that was to come to all of us. Humility is pride's counterpoint and is a necessary virtue to endure suffering. After all, if you don't have humility, how could we ever ask for help along this road to Calvary?

Virtues will be called upon on this road and they don't come immediately; rather, they are forged by trial, error, and repentance. In developing virtues, you have to try and try again to be better than before. This same persistence of the will is needed in dealing with suffering. It prepares our soul for hardship and the individual virtues are equipped and ready for specific trials before us.

CHAPTER 21

Helping Hands

*"And as they led him away, they seized one Simon of
Cyrene, who was coming in from the country, and
laid on him the cross, to carry it behind Jesus."*

—Luke 23:26

There once was a man who was walking back to town
from the countryside, tired and hungry from his travels. He most likely was minding his own business until he
was thrust into the climax of the world's greatest tragedy.
He was approached to help a poor beaten man carry a very
heavy load. He was most likely resistant at first but complied when he saw the man. After all, how could someone
deny helping another who was in such agony? That man was
Simon of Cyrene, and he helped Christ carry his cross.

Simon is mentioned in three of the four Gospels and
only receives one verse in the Passion story. This one verse,
though, is filled with great meaning, showing us that we,
too, will encounter many Simon of Cyrenes in our life as
we carry our cross. We can think of times when we were

111

suffering and comforted by our friends and family. Further-more, when someone randomly may come to our aid. They were on their travels, minding their own business, much like Simon of Cyrene, but God's providence intersected their path with ours just when we needed it most.

One of the hardest things to do when we are suffering is to ask for help. We don't want to inconvenience anyone, and we surely don't want them to suffer alongside us, but we must remember that Jesus had help on the road to Calvary. We are social creatures; we aren't hermits. We live in societies and come together at Mass to grow spiritually. It is only nat-ural for us humans to live in relationships and to offer help and accept help from each other.

If I didn't accept others' help, I would literally not be alive today. Asking for things has always been difficult—I hate that my handicap is so demanding of others and I wish so badly that I could do more, not just for myself, but for oth-ers as well. But this is my life. It's part of the cross I have to bear, but God has sent me help by giving me such an incredible family.

My family has helped me every step along the way. I think of when I would get bronchial infections and would need to drain them. This was no easy process. It required a therapy of rigorous chest-thumping with cupped hands, as well as hanging over a couch. Dad was the primary cupp-handed-thumper-hanger, but others helped as well. Dad would see me struggling to breathe and instead of panicking, he would defuse my fear by making the procedure into a game. He would say, "Are you ready?!" Then he would suspend me over the couch, holding me by the legs as he thumped on the back of my lungs. To most people, it probably would seem somewhat medieval. To me, it was a relief. I loved it! The feeling of not knowing if I could get the air I needed as I gasped and tried to cough is not a pleasant one, or something I care to dwell on. But my father was there in that time to not only physically care for me but to keep things light so that I could emotionally endure the suffering.

Imagine living in a hospital and having the same nurse every day for forty years. Think of the bond you would have with that person, someone who kept you alive through different therapies and treatments. That person is my mother. She fed me, raised me, and cared for me—out of anyone in my entire life, the one person who has carried my cross with me the most was my mother. She suffered with me, and although it is difficult to think of, it is true. She didn't suffer like me, but she did suffer *for* me. She suffered with love for her daughter, and that is a sacrifice that every parent makes for their children. But few parents must do what my mother had to do for so long.

My brothers and sisters have also helped me with my cross in different ways. I recall a treatment called patterning that I had when I came home from the hospital the first time. This was a treatment designed to help stimulate muscles and my brain in a coordinated way so that they can relearn how to work together. The process was as follows: one sibling would hold my head and another sibling would hold each limb. They had to raise my legs and arms and turn my head to the right and to the left in unison. A child like me hated this and made their job very difficult. This was a difficult exercise, so much so that it was how my hips popped out of their sockets. We had to do these exercises five times a day for about two years. They hated it because I hated it so much, but I do think that it had lasting effects. It might be the only reason I am able to use my right side a little bit. Patty, Liz, and Michael were helping with this at ages nine, seven, and five. At such a young age, they were helping their paralyzed sister, even though it was not a pleasant process at all. I imagine they were terrified of hurting me or messing up and also frustrated that they couldn't just go outside to play. Regardless, they held strong and helped me tremendously. My siblings started helping me early in life and they never stopped.

My sisters and brothers helped me develop into the woman I am today. Through my childhood and adolescence, they kept me grounded and never allowed me to feel sorry for myself. They helped me in and out of my chair, they included me in games that I could play, and above all, they loved me as the sister I was and treated me no differently.

Today, my sister Kathy cares for me on a day-in, day-out basis. She accepted me into her home and has cared for me with love every day. This is not a "stay in my guest bedroom" kind of arrangement. When I moved in, her life completely changed. She had to sacrifice so much to have me there with her. My sister, Meg, lives close by and I see her regularly. She has her fair share of sacrifices too (being such a close friend of mine has to be one of them). All of my brothers and sisters, Charlotte, Kathy, David, Spencer, Diane, Fr. Peter, Meg, Mary, Chris, Patty, Liz, Michael, Joe and, of course, Paul, have played the role of Simon of Cyrene in my life, and

I would never have been able to carry my cross to this point without them.

If you don't have a large family like me, maybe there are friends or people you have not met yet that will be your Simon of Cyrene. Help is needed when our cross gets too heavy, and not only is there no shame in asking for help, but we have a *duty* to ask for that help. We are called to carry our cross, so if we find ourselves incapable of doing it alone, we must figure out how to do it with help. I don't know if Jesus could physically get to Golgotha without Simon's help. He had just been scourged, he had a crown of thorns digging into his head, and he was being mocked and ridiculed in front of a laughing crowd. How could any human continue on without help?

Simon of Cyrene represents how we suffer together. Evil attempts to isolate us, and temptations brew when we are alone. Satan doesn't want us to suffer together, because when we do, it becomes for one another. Satan wants us to suffer by ourselves so that we question God and turn against him. One of the greatest defenses against this attack is having a spiritual advisor whom we meet with regularly. I have had a few along the way that have made an incredible impact on me. I find it difficult to have deep spiritual conversations with my siblings, as anyone would. It's hard to disclose our fears, spiritual skepticisms, addictions, and thoughts in a completely honest way when we are trying to maintain an image for them. With a priest, he has heard everything and we can tell him anything. The seal of confession offers this veil of protection that puts us at ease so that we can be more open and honest, addressing the root problem rather than the fringes. We must use this incredible sacrament often so that our heart remains pure and our soul remains clean. With this help and the help of others, we will be able to continue forward toward our Calvary.

CHAPTER 22

The Eucharist—A Perpetual Sacrifice

"The greatest love story of all time is contained in a tiny white host."

—Archbishop Fulton J. Sheen

The greatest day in my life was my First Communion. I wore a white dress and prepared to receive my Lord for the first time. This incredible event would turn out to be quite the ordeal for someone like me though, because the nuns instructed us all to receive the Eucharist in the hand. Surprisingly, they made no exception for me and my handicap. Because my hands are contracted with paralysis, I could not make the proper throne in which to place the Eucharist.

However, instead of allowing me to receive the Eucharist on the tongue, they insisted on separating my fingers to put the Host in my hand. My fervent belief in the presence of Jesus in the Eucharist caused me to panic over the fact that I had to bring him into my mouth on my own. Terrified that I would drop the Host and not be sufficiently strong enough to lift my arm, I said a little prayer to Jesus to help me. I ended up needing Meg's help to raise my hand to my mouth. Unfortunately, the excitement of receiving Jesus for the first time was spoiled by the necessary concentration on the physical effort required. For me, there is something very sacred about the priest placing the Host on my tongue. Receiving it in my hand renders Communion an arduous and stressful struggle as opposed to a comforting joy. Something that is so enjoyable for so many people was mired in such stress. Regardless, my life changed forever that day. I was able to experience the greatest mystery of our Catholic faith.

At the Sacrifice of the Mass, we encounter Jesus Christ fully present—Body, Blood, Soul, and Divinity—in the unleavened bread. As a central dogma of our faith, Catholics believe that Jesus descends upon the altar at the consecration of the Mass when the priest, who acts *in persona Christi* (the person of Christ), puts his hands over the bread and wine and pronounces the words, "And he took bread, and when he had given thanks he broke it and gave it to them, saying, 'This is my body which is given for you. Do this in remembrance of me.' And likewise the cup after supper, saying, 'This cup which is poured out for you is the new covenant in my blood'" (Lk 22:19–20).

The dogma of transubstantiation is a mystery. To the naked eye, it looks like we are just eating a piece of unleavened bread. However, if we use our eyes of faith, we can come to believe that Jesus becomes fully present to us at the moment of the consecration.

With the priest acting *in persona Christi*, we, the faithful, are united to Christ and drawn up to heaven. Therefore, in a sense, we are both on earth and in heaven during every Mass. We may not always feel God's presence in our hearts at every Mass, but this does not mean that he is not there with us. If we truly believed and had clear knowledge, we would be able to see the angels surrounding the altars in our churches and we would see the Holy Trinity and our Lady present. This is the magnitude of the miracle that occurs at each Mass.

When our Lord said, "Do this in remembrance of me," he was calling us to sacrifice after his example. He is calling us to give ourselves for others. We call it *communion*, which points to a spiritual unification. We welcome him into our body and become one with him. Loving our cross carries this same parallel—we must unite ourselves to Jesus on his cross. We must become one with him; only then will our suffering become sacrifice, only then will we be able to endure the evils of this world and embark towards the next.

Holy Adoration is an indispensable part of the spiritual life. It binds our prayer life with the true presence in a way that imitates the Beatific Vision. We will be adoring God in heaven if we are so lucky to make it to his heavenly kingdom. I believe the Eucharist is Jesus. When I receive the Eucharist, I am receiving Jesus into my soul and body. He transforms me. He gives me himself in the Eucharist and in that he spiritually nourishes me and gives me the energy I need to accept and embrace my suffering. Jesus, in that tiny piece of bread, teaches me how to sacrifice for others as he sacrificed himself on the cross and makes himself available through the miracle of transubstantiation in the Mass. Through the Eucharist, he helps me to imitate him. The more I receive him in the Eucharist, the more I will be able to look at suffering as he does—with the eyes of sacrificial love. The Eucharist is the best spiritual medicine one can have. Its power is quite literally infinite, for it *is* God, and he is both omniscient and omnipotent. We draw from the Eucharist the strength needed to persevere on this road to Calvary.

We will need supplies to survive this arduous road, full of hardships and stumbles along the way. We will need a deeply rooted prayer life, virtues to fuel our will and intellect, a support system to help us along our way, and lastly, and most importantly, the Eucharist. Who can help us carry our cross more than Jesus himself?

The Eucharist *is* a sacrifice. The Mass *is* a sacrifice. By attending Mass regularly and coming into a physical and spiritual communion with our Lord, we are able to march with purpose with our cross on our back. We will not fear what lies ahead on this road, we will not look back, we will give our sufferings purpose through love. We will live our Lord's example and die for others as he died for us.

CHAPTER 23

The Corpus and the Cross

"The death of the Lord our God should not be a cause of shame for us; rather, it should be our greatest hope, our greatest glory."

—St. Augustine

As Catholics, it wouldn't be surprising to hear someone say, "What a beautiful crucifix. Is that Spanish or Italian?" We have all seen beautiful crucifixes. Maybe it's one we saw on a pilgrimage, or maybe it's one at our local parish. Someone who is not a Catholic may see it as grotesque—after all, it is the image of a dead man who had been brutally beaten.

But this morbid symbol is one of the most central images of our faith. I believe that it is not just a symbol, though, of what happened on one Friday afternoon in Jerusalem, but it is a foreshadowing of what is to come in our lives. We have a cross marked on our soul, and finding the beauty in that is a difficult task because it's not carved from Italian wood and painted in gold and silver. Rather, it is adorned in pain and suffering. It is soaked with tears and curved to fit our backs.

The image of Jesus hanging on the cross must not *just* be an incredible reminder of how much Jesus loves us. We must look upon it with full knowledge that we too will be bound to our cross and it is necessary for our salvation. When we look upon the cross, remember the last instruction Jesus gave us before he was put to death. "This is my body which is given for you. Do this in remembrance of me" (Lk 22:19).

Protestants do not display the corpse on the cross like Catholics do. Why is that? They focus on the risen Lord and don't relish sacrifice as we do. Protestants don't believe that good works have a bearing on their soul's eternity. Good works are often sacrificial. If sacrifice isn't needed for our salvation, then why did Christ have to die at all? If we were made in his image and likeness, are we not supposed to live as he did? Or did he purchase our eternity so all we have to do now is believe in him, read his word, and wait for death? Sacrifice demands more. It demands that we die for one another and that we spend our days loving each other and putting ourselves last. "So, the last will be first, and the first last" (Mt 20:16). If all we have to do is believe, then we never have to act. And if actions just flow from our belief, then we really don't have free will. The Protestant theologies really get under my skin because they seek to cheapen what I am enduring. I have felt the call from God to live out this handicap. If all I had to do is believe in him, then why would he ever present me with this cross?

Let us not forget the golden rule: "This is my commandment, that you love one another as I have loved you. Greater love has no man than this, that a man lay down his life for his friends" (Jn 15:12–13). Jesus quite literally instructs us with the only commandment he gave us to lay our life down for our friends, for that is the mark of the greatest love. He first told us and then he showed us. For people to ignore that and to not think it has a bearing on our soul is an exercise in selective hearing. Sacrifice is uncomfortable; it is not pleasant, and so people ignore Christ's calling to sacrifice. They run from it and ultimately run from their happiness along with it. John in his first letter reminds us that "by this we know love, that he laid down his life for us; and we ought to lay down our lives for the brethren" (1 Jn 3:16).

Besides our own actions, sacrifice in and of itself is lauded through the Mass. The sacrificial love Jesus has for us, which is re-presented at the Mass, is one of the central mysteries of the faith. He gives us his body and blood to consume so that we can unite ourselves to him. This is quite literally a communion, and it is the central facet of our faith. If I am honest with myself, I can look at a crucifix and say with all certainty, "He knows every human suffering and I am not alone in my pain. He has given me numerous loving people in my life to help me deal with my pain."

We may look upon crosses in our houses and marvel at their beauty—this uplifts our thoughts to the love Christ has for us. We must take it a step further though and contemplate our own cross in light of his. If we ignore or flee from our cross, how can we ever unite it to his? The crucifix serves as a reminder of the price paid for our salvation and of our own suffering to come. This life will beat us up until we take our last breath, but what we are called to give pales in comparison to what our Lord gave. He agonized in the garden; he was scourged and crowned. Beaten and mocked, he carried his cross to be nailed to it. When we see a cross, it must serve as a reminder that Jesus gave everything. His body was broken, yet his spirit was commended into God's hands. He had nothing left to give. We must ask ourselves when we see a crucifix, "How much have I given?" The answer will always be "Not as much as he." It is important to keep the corpus on the cross because it is the image of someone who completely and totally emptied himself out of love for us. How much can we empty of ourselves for him?

In Saint Faustina's diary, she lends us a beautiful perspective on the cross. She speaks about three groups of people and how they handle suffering. The first group is seen as the people dragging their crosses behind them after they have thrown them down. The second group is seen as the ones carrying their crosses, and the third group is seen as the people who hang on the cross. I see myself in the second group of people, but I believe the Lord wants me to be in the third group, one who hangs on the cross out of love for Jesus and others.

This third group is known as the victim souls, the ones who have been chosen by God in a very special way to sacrifice for others. This is a very special group, and Sister Faustina points out that to be in this group requires a lot of faith and trust in God every minute of the day. I think it also takes a great amount of love of God and a deep understanding of the mystery of suffering and sacrificial love in order to want to choose the cross for myself. I will admit that I am not there yet, but I am trying. I believe that I am meant to take my cross an extra step, beyond the average person. I have often called my handicap my vocation—Christ chose me to be a victim soul and this suffering is a major way that I communicate with the Lord. The fact that the cross can be that phone line to heaven is a beautiful concept, and one I don't think most Protestants understand. They seem to forget that there is no Resurrection without the cross.

I recall hearing a story about the famous author Flannery O'Connor. She was at a dinner party one night with a lot of Protestant friends, and as the party continued into the early hours, guests at the party began to speak about religion. They were marveling at how beautiful of a symbol the Eucharist was, for they didn't believe in Christ's true presence in the Eucharist. Ms. O'Connor, in a way that only she could, stepped forward and said, "Well, if it's a symbol, to hell with it."

Of course, this stunned the party, and I am not sure if she was ever invited back. Yet it highlights the depth of our Catholic faith. Our faith goes beyond the symbol. We are meant to unite ourselves with these spiritual realities and transcend this world to receive inklings of the next. How will we ever be able to recognize that heavenly paradise if we maintain a shallow view of our faith? So I ask the Protestant who feels uncomfortable showing our Lord on the cross, "What good is a cross without someone dying on it?"

Prayer for Carrying the Cross

Jesus, I ask you to give me the strength to carry this cross that you have given me out of love for others. I ask you to be my strength in times of weakness. I ask you to be my light in the midst of the darkness of suffering. My humanity is weak, so I ask you to make me strong so that I might be a bold witness to the sacrificial love you display in carrying your cross. Mother Mary, Mother of the suffering Christ, I ask for your motherly protection and grace to carry this cross with you and your Son. I believe in your tender love for me, and I beg you to hear me as I ask for the grace to carry my cross with joy. Amen.

Looking Back

*"All the darkness in the world cannot extinguish
the light of a single candle."*

—St. Francis

I have a picture of me as a child running around and play-ing. I love this picture because it is of a much simpler life. The simple joy that I had shone bright through my toothy smile. I had no idea at the time that I would catch a simple case of chicken pox. And that chicken pox would somehow get into my spine where it would become spinal meningitis. I had no idea that my days of walking were numbered and that God had a very different plan for me than he does for most. I had no idea that I would spend many lonely nights in the hospital fighting for breath and that I would live as a handicapped woman for the remainder of my life. Look-ing back on that little one-year-old, I wouldn't trade places with her. Even through all the suffering related to my hand-icap and the spiritual suffering that followed, I have attained a personal friendship with God that I wouldn't trade for anything. Of course, it could always be better, but I know full well that friendship would not be where it is today if I hadn't carried my cross to this point.

Looking at suffering on a broader timeline is important to try, for it is how God sees it. God is outside of time, thus he can see things unaffected by the moment. He can see the totality of it all. We must strive to do that. When I look back on my life, I see that the constant suffering of my life has strengthened me and called upon my faith daily, leading me to a deeper relationship with God. So, because of that, it has been a great blessing for me.

We need the ability to look beyond the moment, because if we can't, then we will only feel pain and run to self-pity or worldly pleasures for temporary relief. This makes our cross solely about us when it needs to be for others. As I look back on my life, my memories aren't plagued by the difficult times of my life. What I focus on in my memory is lying on the floor playing games with my family or lying on the kitchen table, watching the family move about their day, or lying on a table in the weight room of Ave Maria awaiting them to call my name to give me my diploma. It's easy to pity me, but please do not. My life is filled with as much joy as it is filled with tribulation. This joy is only magnified when I look to my Lord and talk to him.

My relationship with the Lord is direct, open, and honest. We talk every day and I try my best to listen. When I don't get something that I want, I let him know in no uncertain terms. He may say, "Too bad, Therese," or he may say, "Not yet." In turn, I try to understand his plan, but I know I will never be able to completely. Developing this relationship has been the greatest joy in my life. I would never have had this kind of friendship with God if I hadn't suffered and looked up for answers so frequently throughout my life. My cross has put God on speed dial; it is a phone line that he will always answer.

Suffering makes us feel trapped, and we begin to feel like we will never be relieved of the pain. In the words of St. Thérèse of Lisieux, "The world's thy ship not thy home." We must ensure that through this perilous voyage, we are sailing toward God on the horizon. We may feel at times that this ship may capsize, but remember that Jesus calmed the storm for his disciples and will for us as well. One day the sun will rise, and we will not see it set, for the day will stretch into eternity as we pass away and reach our eternal home. But for now, we must take every day as they come and live in love and joy for our opportunity to be with the Lord.

But to attain such a paradise, we must do more than carry our cross. We must love our cross. I obviously wish that I could walk and that these struggles in my life were allevi-ated, so I don't mean *love* in a superficial way. Love is an act of the will. It is a constant decision every day to turn our suffering into a sacrifice for others. Whether that person is a spouse or a child, sacrifice is the mark of true love, and our sacrifices matter and have a spiritual impact on others. This is an amazing aspect of sacrifice—that by it we can partici-pate with Christ in the salvation of others.

Our cross becomes the sacrifice for those we love, just as Jesus was the Sacrificial Lamb on his cross. It is a heavenly gift for us from God Almighty. It allows us to transcend this life by reminding us of our mortality. We must embrace our mortality for it is our passage to meeting our Lord in the next life. Jesus showed us the perfect example of how to love when loving really hurt. He was battered, scourged, humiliated, rejected, and neglected by those who professed to love him deeply. In his humility and deep love for humanity, he chose to accept the physical, emotional, and spiritual burdens of the cross. When he was being mocked and ridiculed, he did not utter a word. When he was nailed to his cross, he forgave his executioners. When he expired, he had nothing left to give. He had given it all to us, and he gave it through a sacrificial love that we are all called to imitate.

Throughout my life, I have learned that suffering can be meritorious when it is united to Jesus's suffering on the cross. Mother Teresa once said, "Suffering is nothing by itself. But suffering shared with the Passion of Christ is a wonderful gift, the most beautiful gift, a token of love." It is a human temptation to try to avoid suffering in our life. Suffering can be scary and unappealing if it is not put into a Christian mind frame. It is not something we can endure alone, and it tries to isolate us from fellow human beings. This makes it all the more important to run to him in these times and remember that we are never alone.

When I meditate on the passion of Jesus, I can come to the conclusion that there is no suffering he did not endure as a man. Therefore, if I cannot trust Jesus, who understands my suffering, then who can I trust? The human tendency, though, is to blame God for human suffering. The question that we always ask ourselves in times of pain is, "How can a loving God allow good people to suffer?" We can answer that question by looking at the life of Jesus, who came to die and rise again to redeem us from sin. Love is sacrificial. If we truly love one another, we will offer our suffering for the good of another, just as Christ did for us. Jesus shows us that our lives can be an offering of love to God and for others. Jesus showed us that the way to heaven is through the cross because by dying to ourselves, we can rise with him in glory.

I have come to understand every day that suffering is a form of sacrificial love that binds me to God and to my neighbor, opening the door to Eternal Life. That door is open for us. Knowing that all we must do is walk through it with our cross should be a tremendous source of joy in our lives. When we see the crosses nailed to our walls, suspended above our altars, and on the end of our rosaries, let us look upon them with joy, for we know that the greatest sacrifice has been paid in love for us. Let us remember our load is light and our Lord will grant us all the strength we need to carry our crosses to Calvary. Let us know we are not alone and every blessing before us is here to aid in this earthly struggle. Let us lift our cross in full acceptance of our Father's providential plan. Let us carry our cross for each other as Christ did for us. And above all, let us love our cross, today and the next, in service to our brothers and sisters, in imitation of our Lord and in pursuit of our eternal home, where we will live in splendor and communion with our heavenly Father.